Panda Books
Beijing Legends

Jin Shoushen (1906-1968) was born into a Manchu family
which had lived for generations in Beijing. After
graduating from Beijing University, where he studied
literature, he taught in different colleges in Beijing. He
made a careful study of the city's history, topography and
customs, and also became an expert on phonology and
traditional Chinese medicine. Over the years he compiled
comprehensive records of anecdotes and legends about
the capital, which he published in magazines and in book
form. He was known as an authority on Beijing.

In his later years he was a member of the Beijing
Federation of Literary and Art Circles and the Beijing
Drama Research Institute.

Panda Books
First edition 1982
Reprint 1985
Copyright 1982 by CHINESE LITERATURE
ISBN 0-8351-1338-8

Published by CHINESE LITERATURE, Beijing (37), China

Distributed by China International Book Trading Corporation
(GUOJI SHUDIAN), P.O. Box 399, Beijing, China

Printed in the People's Republic of China

Jin Shoushen

Beijing Legends

Translated by Gladys Yang

Panda Books

CONTENTS

Preface

THESE folk-tales are translated from *Beijing Legends*, compiled by Jin Shoushen, a Manchu gentleman whose family lived for many generations in Beijing. Based on the tales told him by people from many walks of life in the capital, they were first published in 1957 by the Beijing Publishing House. What they lack in literary polish is made up for by the genuine folk flavour with which they carry us back to the building of Beijing as the Ming capital in 1421. They deal with the city's layout, some of its chief monuments, place names and different legends, and give us fascinating glimpses of the life of rulers as well as ordinary people.

The front cover, the painting of Nezha, was done for Panda Books by the well-known cartoonist Ding Cong. Nezha plays a prominent part in these tales and has a special place in Chinese legend; but his pedigree can be traced back to India. An Indian Buddhist legend describes a young god Nalakuvara or Nalakubala, who was the third son of the Heavenly King Vaisravana, one of the twenty devas. During the Ming Dynasty, this boy's name was transliterated as Nezha, first in Wu Cheng'en's *Pilgrimage to the West* and then in *The Canonization of the Gods*; and his father became Li Jing, an early Tang general who won renown by defeating the Eastern Turks. Because Li Jing helped to build up the Tang Dynasty he became a guardian god.

The Canonization of the Gods attributed great ability to Nezha, who was said to have killed the son of the Dragon King. In revenge, the Dragon King tried to flood the country. In order to clear his father of blame, Nezha disembowelled himself and cut off all his flesh which he derived from his parents; but after his death his divine teacher made him a new body out of a lotus flower, and he became a god. The *Pilgrimage to the West* presents him as one of the gods who defended Heaven and fought with the Monkey King. Because of his supernatural powers and his defiance of the Dragon King, Nezha was a well-loved figure and the people of Beijing were proud to claim his patronage.

Unfortunately many of the temples and pagodas described in these tales have now fallen into ruins. China had such a wealth of old relics, and such limited funds for their upkeep, that they were not carefully treasured. Thus the capital's city wall and most ornamental archways were pulled down after Liberation to facilitate traffic and, for a lover of history, the face of old Beijing is sadly changed. All the more reason then, to preserve these legends describing its past; and it is heartening to see that today the People's Government is taking steps to restore old monuments.

Half a million years ago, in the days of Beijing Man, this area was largely under water. This old folk memory seems to be embodied in the name Bitter Sea Waste. Beijing knows climatic extremes, a blazing summer and a freezing winter. Its people were never accustomed to the softer ways of living in the south, for drought, high winds and sandstorms constantly threatened the city. Hence the many stories of wicked dragons — the lords controlling water — who are presented as trying to take over Beijing.

Emperors, their advisers and ministers figure in some of these stories, seen from the viewpoint of the man in the street as a grasping, tyrannical, incompetent lot. They have no idea, for instance, how to design the corner towers of the Forbidden City: the plan for these is copied from a pedlar's cricket cage. And so, as in most folk stories of other lands, the real heroes are the resourceful working people who retain their self-respect and sense of humour through natural calamities, man-made disasters and countless political changes.

Gladys Yang

The Eight-Armed Nezha City

EVERYONE calls Beijing the Eight-armed Nezha City.* They say only eight-armed Nezha could have subdued the vicious dragons in Bitter Sea Waste. Well, how did Beijing come to be built as an Eight-armed Nezha City? There's a folk-tale about this.

The Emperor decided to build a northern capital, Beijing,** and entrusted this task to the Minister of Works. That threw the minister into a panic. He promptly petitioned the throne: "Beijing was originally known as the Bitter Sea Waste, and the dragons there are too vicious for your humble subject to overcome. I beg Your Majesty to send some military advisers instead!"

The Emperor saw reason in this. Beijing could only be built by a genius with knowledge of heaven and earth, who knew the ways of both the spirits above and

---

* Nezha, a mythical boy with supernatural powers, killed the son of the Dragon King. Later he disembowelled himself and cut the flesh from his bones; but his spirit took the form of a lotus, and he continued to battle with and overcome many evil spirits.

** The inner city of Beijing was built in 1267 in the Yuan Dynasty. In 1368, when the Ming Dynasty was established, the north wall was pulled down and rebuilt five *li* to the south. In 1419, the south wall was pulled down and rebuilt more than a *li* farther south, forming the inner city as we know it today. The outer city wall was built in 1553.

the devils below. So he asked his advisers, "Which of you can go and build a northern capital for me?"

His advisers eyed each other, not daring to utter a word, until finally someone really had to answer and Chief Adviser Liu Bowen volunteered, "I'll go!"

At once Deputy Adviser Yao Guangxiao volunteered, "And so will I."

The Emperor was pleased, sure that these two outstanding advisers had the ability to overcome dragons and tigers. He forthwith sent them off to build Beijing.

Liu Bowen and Yao Guangxiao took the imperial edict and travelled to the Waste where Beijing now stands. After putting up in a hostel, they went out every day to survey the terrain and figure out how to build the city in such a way that the dragons could not make trouble. However, Chief Adviser Liu and Deputy Adviser Yao had nothing but contempt for each other.

"Deputy Adviser Yao," proposed Liu, "let's live apart, you in the west city, I in the east. Each of us must think up a plan, then in ten days' time we'll meet and, sitting back to back, draw our plans for the city. Then we'll compare the two to see if they tally."

Yao Guangxiao knew perfectly well that Liu Bowen hoped to shine and hog all the credit.

"Very well," he said with a grim smile. "You're right, chief adviser, that's what we should do."

So the two advisers split up. For the first couple of days, although the two of them were staying apart and neither went out to survey the terrain, both heard a voice saying, "Just copy me and you'll do fine." The voice sounded like a child's, and the words were clearly repeated time and again. Who could the speaker be?

There was no one to be seen. "Just copy me" — what did that mean? Neither adviser could make head or tail of this.

On the third day they both went out to survey the terrain again. Wherever Adviser Liu went he saw a child in a red jacket and short pants walking ahead of him. When Liu speeded up, so did the child; when he slowed down, so did the child. At first he paid no special attention to this, but then he started wondering about it. He deliberately stood still. Ah! How extraordinary! So did the child. Liu couldn't for the life of him think what the boy was up to.

How about Deputy Adviser Yao? He saw a child like that too, and couldn't for the life of him think what the boy was up to.

Back in their different hostels, again both advisers heard a voice in their ears. "Just copy me and you'll do fine." Liu in the east city and Yao in the west city wondered: Can this child in the red jacket and short pants be Nezha? Doesn't seem like him. Nezha was supposed to have eight arms. Liu in the east city and Yao in the west city came to the same decision: If I meet that boy tomorrow, I'll have a good look at him.

The next day, the fourth day after they had reached their agreement, Liu Bowen went out after breakfast for a stroll with an attendant. Why take an attendant today? So that the attendant could help him see if it was Nezha. Yao Guangxiao in the west city had the same idea. Both men had heard the same voice, seen the same child, and today they saw him again. Still wearing a red jacket and short pants, but not the same jacket as the previous day: this one was more like a cape with a lotus-leaf edge, and from the two shoulders dangled soft silken fringes which rustled in the wind like arms. At the sight of them Liu suspected that this must be Eight-armed Nezha. He hurried forward to catch hold of the child and have a closer look; but the faster he chased him the faster the child ran away, repeating, "Just copy me and you'll do fine!" Then he made off and vanished completely.

When Liu's attendant saw him chasing down the road, he did not know what was up. He called after him, "Commander! Commander! Why are you running?"

Liu stopped to ask him, "Did you see a child in a red jacket and short pants?"

"Not I," said the attendant. "All this time I've been following you I haven't seen a soul."

Then Liu Bowen knew for sure that it was Nezha.

As for Yao Guangxiao, exactly the same thing had happened to him.

The two commanders went back to their hostels. Liu thought: "Copy me" must mean draw a plan of a city like Eight-armed Nezha, so as to keep down the dragons in Bitter Sea Waste. Fine! Let's see how you handle this, Yao Guangxiao. If you can't produce such a plan, you're not fit to be imperial adviser! Yao in the west city was thinking at the same time: Now we'll soon see you lose your title "Chief Adviser"!

On the ninth day Liu sent word to Yao: "At noon tomorrow, in the centre of the city, we'll draw our plans back to back. Please be there on time." And Yao agreed to this.

At noon on the tenth day, in a big empty square in the centre of the town, two tables and two chairs were

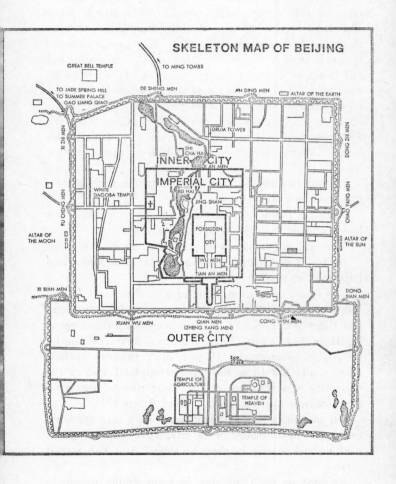

SKELETON MAP OF BEIJING

GREAT BELL TEMPLE

TO MING TOMBS

TO JADE SPRING HILL
TO SUMMER PALACE
GAO LIANG QIAO

DE SHENG MEN

AN DING MEN

ALTAR OF THE EARTH

XI ZHI MEN

DRUM TOWER

DONG ZHI MEN

SHI
CHA HAI

INNER CITY

DI AN MEN

IMPERIAL CITY

WHITE
DAGOBA TEMPLE

BEI HAI

JING SHAN

FU CHENG MEN

CHAO YANG MEN

ALTAR OF
THE MOON

FORBIDDEN
CITY

WU MEN

ALTAR OF
THE SUN

TIAN AN MEN

XI BIAN MEN

DONG
BIAN MEN

XUAN WU MEN

QIAN MEN
(ZHENG YANG MEN)

CONG WEN MEN

OUTER CITY

TEMPLE OF
AGRICULTURE

TEMPLE OF
HEAVEN

set out, the chairs back to back, and the two advisers arrived.

Liu asked, "Which way do you want to face, deputy adviser?"

Yao answered, "You live in the east city, chief adviser, so you should sit facing east. Your younger brother will sit facing west."

When they had taken their seats, attendants supplied them with paper, brushes, ink and inkstones. They picked up the brushes and stroke by stroke drew their plans. Just before sunset both finished their plans of the city, and each picked up the other's to examine it. Then both of them burst out laughing, because their plans were identical, each being an Eight-armed Nezha City.

Yao Guangxiao asked the chief adviser to explain his Eight-armed Nezha City.

Liu said, "This gate in the centre due south is Zheng Yang Men, Nezha's head. A head should have two ears, and those are the gates to its east and west. The two wells inside Zheng Yang Men are his eyes. On the east side, the Cong Wen Men, Dong Bian Men, Chao Yang Men and Dong Zhi Men are four of Nezha's arms. On the west side of the Zheng Yang Men, the Xuan Wu Men, Xi Bian Men, Fu Cheng Men and Xi Zhi Men are Nezha's other four arms. The An Ding Men and De Sheng Men in the north are his feet."

Yao Guangxiao nodded, saying, "Yes, of course. But does Nezha have only eight arms, no heart, liver, spleen, lungs or kidneys?"

Liu Bowen's face turned red. "Of course he has!" he retorted. "How could a dead Nezha keep down vicious dragons?" He pointed irately at his plan.

Zheng Yang Men

"Look, brother. The rectangular Imperial City is
Nezha's viscera, and Tian An Men at its entrance is
the way into his viscera and leads in the other direction
to Zheng Yang Men, his brain. The long, level road
between them is Nezha's gullet."

With a laugh Yao Guangxiao drawled, "Don't get
het-up, chief adviser. I can see your plan is most carefully worked out. The two roads running south and
north on both sides of the viscera are Nezha's main
ribs, and the alleys branching off are his lesser ribs —
right? You've really worked it out to the last detail!"

Although provoked, Liu Bowen had to keep his
temper. At any rate, the plan for an Eight-armed
Nezha City had been drawn, and neither adviser could
hog all the credit. Chief Adviser Liu did not mind

about this, but Deputy Adviser Yao became so cast down that he went off to live as a monk, waiting to see how Liu would build Beijing.

What Liu Bowen did not foresee was that the building of Beijing would enrage the vicious dragons, which led to "Gao Ling's Race for Water" and many other stories.

How the Black Rock
Went to Lu Gou Qiao

"THE Big Black Rock made no move; the Second Black Rock would only budge; the Third Black Rock went to Lu Gou Qiao."* This is another story about how Liu Bowen built Beijing. The local people say he "created" Beijing, but we say he "built" the city. Still, what has this to do with the Black Rock? Another legend tells us.

After Liu Bowen and Yao Guangxiao each succeeded in drawing a plan of Beijing, Yao, being narrow-minded, went off in a huff to become a monk, so we can pass over him. Chief Adviser Liu was a wise man. He determined to build Beijing as an Eight-armed Nezha City. He thought: I can do this, that's certain; but will it really keep down the vicious dragons in this Bitter Sea Waste? This troubled the canny adviser. After thinking over the problem for two days, he learned that on Shangfang Mountain in the county of Fangshan there were three big black rocks which had attained sainthood, one for ten thousand years, the second for five thousand years and the third for a thousand

---

* The construction of Lu Gou Qiao, sometimes called Marco Polo Bridge, began in 1187 in the Jin Dynasty. The stone lions on the balustrades were added in 1444 under the Ming. The town of Fei east of the bridge was built in 1640.

years; so they were able to subdue dragons and tigers. He thought: If I could get hold of one of those rocks with divine power, I'd surely be able to keep down the dragons. If I could get that Big Black Rock which has attained sainthood for ten thousand years, the dragons of Bitter Sea Waste would never be able to rampage again or stage another come-back. But how to get such a heavy rock, and one with such divine powers, down to Beijing? I must find some way by combining soft and hard tactics.

Before telling you what his tactics were, I should say that the three brothers the Big Black Rock, the Second Black Rock and the Third Black Rock on Shangfang Mountain knew what Liu Bowen was scheming.

The Third Black Rock said, "Who wants to go? I'm sitting pretty here."

The Second Black Rock said, "I'm not going either. I'm not taking orders from Crooked Nose Liu Bowen."

The Third Black Rock said, "Who wants to go? I'm only afraid Crooked Nose may use violence to make me."

"Just let him try!" growled the Big Black Rock.

Liu Bowen, having made up his mind to shift these three sacred rocks, decided to use dual tactics. First he would prepare incense and offerings and, taking a retinue, would invite the three sacred rocks down with great pomp and ceremony. If that failed, he had another trick up his sleeve. He'd keep heavenly troops hidden in the seams of his sleeves to frighten the Big Black Rock, the Second Black Rock and the Third Black Rock into coming quietly down from the hill.

After making these preparations, Liu Bowen set out with an imposing retinue to invite the three sacred rocks

down to the city.   They went southwest from Beijing,
crossed Lugou Ford and made straight for Shangfang
Mountain.   When they reached its foot, Liu Bowen
dropped his chief adviser's swagger and went up very
earnestly to the three sacred rocks.   After lighting incense and presenting offerings, he said most reverently,
"Respected Sacred Rocks, in accordance with the Emperor's edict, I, Liu Bowen, have come to beg you to
honour Beijing with your presence.   Then the Emperor
will confer on each of you the title Commander of the
Realm!"

The Big Black Rock lay there quietly and made no
move. Seeing this, the Second Black Rock and the
Third Black Rock thought: Since Big Brother hasn't
moved, we needn't either.

When Liu Bowen saw that his incense and offerings
had not done the trick, and the rocks had snubbed him
like this, he decided to get tough.   He whispered to
the heavenly troops up his sleeve, "I shall have to trouble you to drive these three rascally rocks to Beijing.
Then the Emperor is sure to ennoble you!"

With a cry of assent the heavenly troops flew out
from the seams of his sleeves, brandishing swords, spears
and halberds. They surrounded the three sacred rocks
and yelled: "Get moving, quick, to Beijing!"

Still the Big Black Rock made no move. The Second
Black Rock was scared into budging. The Third Black
Rock, powerless to resist this show of might, had to
leave his two elder brothers and go down the hill.   Liu
Bowen saw he could not shift the Big Black Rock and
the Second Black Rock, but at least he had the Third
Black Rock to show that he had carried out his im-

perial mission, and so he went down the mountain with
his attendants to drive the Third Black Rock to Beijing.

Now for a slight digression. When Liu Bowen had
crossed Lugou Ford, the Dragon King there had heard
of his plan from Prince Dragon, son of the Dragon
King of Bitter Sea Waste, and they had discussed how
to block the Third Black Rock's way to Beijing. They
decided to build a scorpion city at the ford, so that
when Liu Bowen drove the Third Black Rock there
the scorpion could sting him and stop him from going
any farther. First they built the scorpion's tail, Lu Gou
Qiao, which was finished overnight. Then they built
its body, the town of Fei east of the bridge, with two
wells outside its east gate as the scorpion's eyes. A

Lu Gou Qiao (Marco Polo Bridge)

little farther east stood two mounds, one north and one south, and these were the scorpion's front pincers. No sooner was this Scorpion City completed than Liu Bowen came along driving the Third Black Rock.

His attendants reported, "Adviser, when we came this way there was no bridge over Lugou Ford. Now there's not only a long stone bridge, there's a city as well to its east. Please take a look, sir."

Liu Bowen heard this with dismay, and spurred his horse to the bridge to investigate. He realized that this Scorpion City would try to prevent Third Black Rock from reaching Beijing. Still, there was nothing for it but to press on.

With a show of calm he said, "Never mind, let's cross this bridge of ours."

He drove the Third Black Rock on again. But the Third Black Rock stopped dead at the west end of the bridge. Then Liu Bowen secretly ordered his heavenly troops to drive the rock on, and told him, "Hurry up, Third Commander. Once across this river we'll soon reach Beijing. Then the Emperor will grant you a title!"

Then the Third Black Rock had to trundle on till he had lumbered over Lu Gou Qiao. Liu Bowen decided not to go through the town over the scorpion's back — that was too risky! So he skirted south of it, driving the rock, to keep out of the scorpion's way so the Third Black Rock would not be stung to death. Suddenly, however, the scorpion's tail lashed round and stung the Third Black Rock — he could never move again.

Liu Bowen sighed, "Confound it! Beijing may not be flooded, but both banks of this Lugou Ford quite likely will be!" So he had to think of another way of curbing those vicious dragons.

Ever since this black rock appeared south of the town of Fei, the local people have told this story describing how "the Big Black Rock made no move; the Second Black Rock would only budge; the Third Black Rock went to Lu Gou Qiao."

Gao Liang's Race for Water

HUNDREDS of thousands of years ago, so the old folk in Beijing say, this place was in a bad way because it was a briny sea known as Bitter Sea Waste; and people had to live in the western and northern hills, leaving the Bitter Sea to the Dragon King. The Dragon King, his wife, son, daughter-in-law and grandchildren lorded it over the Bitter Sea so that the local people who had taken to the hills lived a wretched life. How wretched was their life? They used the earth as their cauldrons and weighed out their firewood in bushels.

Some years later a boy called Nezha appeared in a red jacket and short pants. He had real ability. Coming to the Bitter Sea he fought the Dragon King for nine times nine days, eighty-one days in all. He captured the Dragon King and his wife, while their son, daughter-in-law and grandchildren fled. After the capture of the Dragon King the water slowly ebbed away and soil emerged. Nezha sealed up the different outlets to the sea, sealing up the Dragon King and his wife in a large lake, then built a big white pagoda on top so that ever after they had to stay there to guard it.

Now that the water had ebbed away, the name Bitter Sea was changed to the Waste. As time went by people built houses there and settled down there. Villages sprang up, as well as market-towns. By now the dragon's son who had fled had become the king, and he and his wife took refuge with their son and daughter in a lake at the foot of the western hills. There they lay low, keeping quiet. When they saw the people of Bitter Sea Waste increasing from day to day, that increased their exasperation. They kept wanting to go out and rampage, to flood this Waste which was no longer called the Bitter Sea.

One day the new Dragon King heard that a city called Beijing was to be built in the Waste. That really enraged him. He thought: You people razed our Dragon Palace, and now you want to build a city there just to infuriate me! Then came word that Liu Bowen and Yao Guangxiao had back to back drawn a plan of Beijing — an Eight-armed Nezha City with eight gates — and its construction had already started.

The Dragon King told his wife, "Confound it! How maddening! If they build an Eight-armed Nezha City, we've no hope of making a come-back!"

"Never mind," said his wife. "Let them build their city. We'll stay here in our Dragon Palace and keep out of trouble."

The Dragon King stamped his foot. "That's no way to talk," he fumed. "How can I watch them sitting pretty! I must seize this chance, before their city is finished, to drain away all its water. Then before they can finish it they'll die of thirst!"

His wife, unable to talk him out of this, had to go along with him.

Having hatched their plot, the next day at dawn they set out with their son and daughter and a wheelbarrow loaded with vegetables. They had dressed like peasants going to the market in town. The Dragon King pushed the barrow, his wife pulled the loop in front, and with their children following some way behind they sneaked into Beijing. Of course the Dragon King had no intention of selling vegetables. He found an out-of-the-way spot and dumped them all there. Then he, his wife, Dragon Boy and Dragon Girl went round the town according to their plan. Dragon Boy drank all the sweet water there, Dragon Girl all the bitter water; then they changed themselves into two fish-scale water-panniers and lay down one on each side of the wheel-barrow. With the Dragon King pushing and his wife pulling it, they went out of Xi Zhi Men bold as brass.

Meantime what of Liu Bowen? Now that the Eight-armed Nezha City had been built, he had taken his inspectors to supervise the building of the imperial palace. Suddenly someone dashed over covered with sweat. "Report, chief adviser!" he shouted. "We're in big trouble. Every single well, large or small, in Beijing is dry. What's to be done!"

Liu Bowen was flabbergasted. Then he figured: Everyone knows that the Dragon King, his wife and their son Prince Dragon are jealous of this city. Because of course once it's built, that tribe of dragons can never make a come-back. He promptly sent subordinates to all the city gates to investigate and find out from the wardens if any suspicious characters had been through their gates that day. Horsemen galloped off to carry out his orders. Very soon they came back and reported that the only suspicious characters to leave the city had gone through Xi Zhi Men. One of them reported, "An old hunchback was seen at Xi Zhi Men pushing a wheelbarrow, with an old woman tugging in front. On the barrow were two dripping fish-scale water-panniers. They left by Xi Zhi Men an hour ago."

The warden added, "They were such strange fish-scale panniers that I had a good look at them. They weren't too big, yet that old fellow was sweating as he pushed the barrow."

Liu Bowen nodded. "The vicious old dragon!" he said. "We'll just have to send someone to catch him and bring back the water."

The chief inspector asked, "How can we do that?"

Liu told him, "It'll be hard or easy, depending on how you look at it. Hard, because if that damned dragon sees someone after him, he'll swamp him with water to drown him. Easy, because if our man spears the fish-

Xi Zhi Men

scale panniers then dashes straight back without looking round no matter if all hell breaks loose behind, once he reaches Xi Zhi Men he'll be safe and sound."

His men shook their heads saying, "That's a tall order. Not easy."

Liu stamped impatiently. "There's no time to be lost! We can't wait for that damned dragon to empty all that water down his lake, or we'll never get it back. Who'll take this on?"

His officers, high and low, eyed each other in silence. The chief adviser was frantic! Then they heard a clear voice ring out:

"Let me go, sir. I promise to catch up with the damned dragon and to spear the fish-scale panniers. I guarantee to bring the water back."

Liu saw it was a builder in his twenties, big-eyed and alert-looking.

"What's your name?" he asked, very pleased.

"I'm Gao Liang, a mason working on the palace."

Liu nodded and promptly took a red-tasselled spear from the weapon rack. He handed it to Gao Liang, saying, "Be very careful. I'll take troops up the West Gate to back you up."

Gao Liang took the spear, promising, "You can count on me, sir." Then without one backward glance he flew off in pursuit of the dragon.

Once out of Xi Zhi Men a dilemma faced him. To the north was a road to the northwest, leading to Jade Spring Hill. To the west was a road to the southwest, leading to the western hills. To the south was a road south to Fu Cheng Men. Which way should he go? He must make a lightning decision. He thought: Didn't Liu Bowen say that damned dragon is taking the water to his lake? The only lake is at Jade Spring Hill. I'll catch him before he gets there. He sprinted off to the northwest, gripping his spear, his eyes flashing fire. Before long he came to a gully between two high banks, just wide enough for a wheelbarrow to pass through, but too narrow for a horsecart. There were roads on both sides, however. Would the dragons have taken one of them? On one bank some peasants were talking.

One said, "Very odd they were, those two water-panniers glinting like the scales of a fish or dragon."

"Beats me," said another. "With all that sweet water in Jade Spring, why lug those two panniers of water northwest?"

Another said, "That old fellow and his wife were puffing and blowing, lugging that barrow of water so fast through our gully. At their age too — they're really tough!"

Gao Liang knew then that the dragons had headed northwest. Without a word, gripping his spear, he hurried northwest through the gully. Before long the road forked in front of a willow copse. Which way had the dragons gone? He was at a loss when he heard some boys in the copse.

"Hey, big brother with the tasselled spear, give us a drill!" one called to him.

Gao Liang saw some small boys beneath the trees clapping their hands and grinning. His spirits rose. He told them, "Little brothers, I'll drill you presently. First tell me if an old man and old woman passed here pushing a wheelbarrow."

"They took that track to the left," the little boys chorused.

Thanking them, he set off again. Later on this place was given the name Big Willows.

Hurrying on in pursuit, Gao Liang came to a pool that had dried up. Its banks were spattered with water, and in the bed of the pool was a rut made by a barrow. At once he understood: This must have been a pond. That damned dragon's barrow stopped here and he didn't leave a single drop of water — he carried it all away! Later this place was given the name South Hollow.

Planting his spear in the ground, Gao Liang vaulted over the pond and hurried on, eager to get back the water for the city. Before long he came to another pond — later called Middle Hollow — with a deep rut made by the barrow and many footprints. He realized that the dragons must be tired; why else should they have left so many deep footprints? If he put on a spurt he could certainly catch up. He bounded forward, and very soon the Jade Spring Hill came into sight. Gao Liang strained his eyes. In the distance, sure enough, was a barrow loaded with two water-panniers. An old hunchback and an old woman were seated on the ground mopping their sweaty faces. They must be the Dragon King and his wife, quite worn out. Gao Liang exulted, his heart going pit-a-pat. He ducked into a field of sorghum to make a detour to the back of the dragons, then sprang up and speared one of the fish-scale panniers. Water came flooding out. But before he could spear the second, it changed into a pot-bellied youngster who dived into the Jade Spring. The dragon's wife picked up the pannier Gao Liang had speared, and flew over the peak of the north hill to escape to Black Dragon Lake. All these things happened at once, as fast as lightning. Before Gao Liang could decide what to do, the Dragon King roared, "You've ruined my grand scheme, damn you! Don't think you can get away."

With a start Gao Liang took to his heels, pursued by what sounded like a racing tide. When he speeded up, so did the water; when he slowed down, it slowed down too. Now Xi Zhi Men came in sight, and he could distinctly see Liu Bowen above it. In his relief he forgot himself and looked round, and the water swept him away.

Since then there has been water in Beijing's wells, but most of it is brackish. What of the sweet water? It was carried off by Dragon Boy to Jade Spring Hill. And the Dragon King? That's another story. Later, over the place where Gao Liang drowned, men built the Gao Liang Qiao.* People seeing this stone bridge may pass on this story.

---

* A stream flows from the Jade Spring past Kunming Lake to the canal, formerly known as Gaoliang Stream, which runs southeast past the Zoo and the back of the Exhibition Hall, then east to Gao Liang Qiao. For thousands of years this was Beijing's main waterway, and before the Yongding River was diverted here, it was Beijing's main source of water.

Bei Xin Qiao—New North Bridge

IN Beijing, a road four or five *li* long runs from Dong Zhi Men to the Drum Tower, and another ten *li* long from Cong Wen Men in the south to the north city wall. These roads intersect at Bei Xin Qiao (New North Bridge). But in fact there is no bridge there, no balustrade either. There's another folk-tale about this.

In the Temple of Yue Fei at Bei Xin Qiao is a well where a dragon is imprisoned. At the time of his imprisonment there he was told, "There's a bridge here which you must guard. When the bridge is old and a balustrade is built, you can come out."

Since then the place has been called Bei Xin Qiao, (New North Bridge) but this "bridge" can never grow old. When grandads tell children this story about the dragon's imprisonment they always add, "This is a true story. My grandad heard from his grandad that in his time a stupid young fellow was curious to see what the dragon looked like; so he started to haul up its chain. When he had hauled it half-way up and the chain lay all over the ground, he heard from the well what sounded like a howling wind, rushing water and the bellowing of an ox. In a fright he let go of the chain, which clattered back into the well. After that no one dared to haul it up again. This is a true story, children." Many, many old folk told this story. I'm repeating it as it was told to me.

This story is the sequel to "Gao Liang's Race for Water". Didn't Gao Liang spear the water-pannier into which Dragon Girl had turned? Dragon Mother carried her wounded daughter over the northern hills to Black Dragon Lake, where the two of them settled down. There are still strange little fish in that lake which dash themselves against stones. The story-tellers say these are Dragon Mother's descendants. As for the Dragon King, after Gao Liang speared the pannier didn't he race after him in a rage with a flood of water? When Gao Liang had been drowned the water subsided. The Dragon King nearly choked with anger, but not daring to provoke Liu Bowen he took Dragon Boy with the sweet water in his belly and dived down to the bottom of the Jade Spring. That's why there is so much water, such sweet water, on Jade Spring Hill. The Dragon King swore to himself: "Liu Bowen! Liu Bowen! I'm going to get even with you, just you wait! When you've finished building Beijing you'll have to leave, and then I can have my own way." So the Dragon King and Dragon Boy settled down below the Jade Spring.

The days and months slipped by till Beijing with its eight gates was completed. Before going back to report this to the Emperor, Liu Bowen remembered the wicked dragon. He thought: Once I'm gone, that brute may run amok again. If Yao Guangxiao were in charge here that would be better, but he's gone off to be a monk. What's to be done? He went in search of Yao, and tracked him down in a temple outside the Southwest Gate. Liu Bowen explained why he had come. "The two of us drew up the plan for this Eight-armed Nezha City," he told him. "When I go back to report, I shall say that both of us built Beijing, and you were the deputy adviser."

Yao Guangxiao agreed to take charge then. And Liu Bowen packed up and left Beijing with his attendants, to go and report back to the Emperor.

When the Dragon King heard that Liu Bowen had gone a long way away, he took Dragon Boy along underground streams to Beijing. Finding a vent, they butted up against it, but it was no use — there was a weight on top. They not only failed to break through but raised big bumps on their heads. How the Dragon King hated Liu Bowen! By the time he and Dragon Boy had butted against several vents their heads were sore and swollen, yet still they had failed to get out.

One day they came to the northeast part of Beijing and saw another vent. The Dragon King and Dragon Boy charged at it. And this time, to their surprise, they broke their way out. The story-tellers say this place was today's Bei Xin Qiao. The Dragon King transformed himself into an old man, Dragon Boy into a lad, and they took a spate of sea water up with them. In a flash, north, south, east and west of Bei Xin Qiao were flooded. The people living there cried to high heaven, while the Dragon King and Dragon Boy sloshed about on the flood, immensely pleased with themselves.

This was reported at once to Deputy Adviser Yao. He said to himself: Liu Bowen is really smart. He guessed that these dragons would run amok, and they have. Yao changed his clothes and, taking a double-edged sword, fairly flew to Bei Xin Qiao. With three sweeps of his sword he stemmed the flood and stopped it from spreading. Then he leapt on to the water, roaring, "Damned dragon, how dare you flood Beijing! The deputy adviser will teach you a good lesson!"

The Dragon King was taken aback. He thought: Liu Bowen isn't in Beijing. Where has this deputy adviser sprung from? He's really tough. With that double-edged sword of his he's stopped the flood. We must guard against him. He signalled to Dragon Boy, and they drew their black dragon swords. Without a word they fell fiercely upon Yao Guangxiao. He swiftly parried their thrusts. Cold steel flashed as the three of them battled together. Yao could have got the better of the Dragon King alone, could easily have captured Dragon Boy alone; but he was no match for father and son together. His sword thrusts slowed down, it seemed he would be worsted, but just as it came to the pinch there was a flash, and with a howl the Dragon King fell flat on the water, blood streaming from his leg. This took place so fast, fast as lightning, that Yao didn't know what had happened and Dragon Boy was stunned. Yao was trying to see who had come to his rescue, when he heard a shout:

"Adviser Yao, hurry up and catch the little dragon! I'm Yue Fei* of the great Song Dynasty."

Joyfully striking out at Dragon Boy, Yao cried, "Please wait, General Yue Fei!"

Yue Fei did not answer. Dragon Boy, rooted to the spot, was cut down. Then Yao locked up both dragons, and at once the water north, south, east and west of the place ebbed away, never to flood again.

Having locked up both dragons, Yao did not know

---

* An ancient general well-known for his courage and loyalty, who was killed at the order of the Emperor on a false charge.

where to put them. After thinking it over he hit on a good plan: he would imprison the Dragon King in the Bei Xin Qiao sea outlet, sinking a deep well there, and fastening him up with a long, long chain. Over the well he would build a large three-roomed temple; but what shrine should be set up there? Why, of course, a shrine to Yue Fei who had helped him capture the Dragon King.

When the Dragon King was chained and about to be thrown in the well, he asked, "Adviser Yao, you're not going to shut me up for ever, are you? When can I come out again?"

"Just wait till this bridge is old and a balustrade's built over it, then you can come out," Yao told him.

After that the place became known as Bei Xin Qiao (New North Bridge) and no balustrade was built there.

Yao imprisoned Dragon Boy in the vent under Diao Bridge by Congwen Gate.

Dragon Boy also asked, "Commander Yao, you're not going to shut me up for ever, are you? When can I come out again?"

"When you hear the iron clapper struck to open the city gate, you can come out."

After that, instead of sounding an iron clapper when Congwen Gate was opened or closed, a bell was struck instead. All the old people say, "Beijing's inner city has nine gates, eight iron clappers and one bell." When people see the Temple to Keep Down the Sea still standing at Bei Xin Qiao, they tend to believe this legend.

The Centipede Wells

FOR many years most of Beijing's well water was brackish. There was precious little sweet water, so that people loved to have even one sip of it. So we have this story about the centipede wells.

Wasn't Beijing an Eight-armed Nezha City? After Gao Liang raced for water, didn't all the city's wells turn brackish? Apart from the Emperor's household, which sent water-carts every day to Jade Spring Hill for sweet water,* the officials high and low and the common people had to make do with brackish water. Drinking brackish water day in, day out was so tiresome that the teahouses had hardly any customers.

One day, after a teahouse had opened, as nobody came to drink tea the shopkeeper sat dozing behind his table when suddenly a customer came in.

"Hey, master, have you boiling water?" he asked.

The shopkeeper opened his eyes and saw an old man dressed in rags. Still, he was pleased to have a customer. He promptly answered, "Yes, the kettle's on the boil. Would you like some tea, sir?"

"Brew me a pot."

The shopkeeper agreed and fetched a teapot, bowl

---

* The palace's water-cart fetched water from Jade Spring Hill till the end of the Qing Dynasty.

and tea-leaves. Having rinsed the teapot and bowl, he brewed the old man some tea. When it had stood for a while, the old man poured himself a bowl. That tea really looked like red soup. The old man shook his head, raised the bowl, sipped the tea, then put the bowl down again.

"Why, master," he asked, "what makes this tea so bitter?"

The shopkeeper sighed, then explained, "Beijing has no sweet water. It was all carried off by the Dragon King. It's a big headache for everyone in the city!"

The old man said with a chuckle, "If you had sweet

Centipede Well

water you wouldn't brew tea with brackish water, would you?"

"We certainly wouldn't."

The old man nodded. From his sleeve he produced a gold centipede just over three inches long, with gold feelers, gold eyes and eighteen legs. He whispered something to it, as if consulting it, and the centipede first shook its head, then nodded. Finally the old man cried, "Off you go then!" The centipede arched its back and flew up into the air, disappearing from sight. The owner of the teahouse watched in amazement, not knowing what was happening. And the old man did not explain, just paid for his tea and left.

Two days later the owner of the teahouse heard that to the east of the Forbidden City a spring of sweet water had gushed out and a well had been sunk there — the one in Da Tian Shui Jing (Big Sweet Well Alley) off Wang Fu Jing.* The shopkeeper was pleased but thought no more about it. Three days later he heard that two more sweet springs had gushed out less than a li outside An Ding Men, and two wells had been sunk there, the Upper and Lower Dragon Wells in Upper Dragon Courtyard.** Again the shopkeeper was pleased but thought no more about it.

Then, five, seven or nine days later, the shopkeeper heard that in the eighteen villages of Fengtai, to the left of each village temple, sweet springs had gushed

---

* In the Ming Dynasty this well was in the Tenth Prince's Mansion. So the street was called Wang Fu Jing (Prince's Mansion Well). During the Qing Dynasty, so old folk say, the water was sold to high officials only and they paid as much as a silver ingot a day.

** Up to the time of the War of Resistance Against Japan, most of the water from these wells was bought by well-to-do families.

out and eighteen wells had been sunk.* This time, apart from feeling pleased, he mulled the business over. Since Liu Bowen built Beijing as an Eight-armed Nezha City, there was never a well of sweet water inside or outside it, he thought. Where have all these wells come from in the last few days? He found it very mysterious.

Later on, when his customers were chatting away as they sipped tea brewed with sweet water, the shop-keeper told them about the old man with the gold centipede, and they marvelled too but were equally mystified.

Some time afterwards one smart fellow said, "These must be centipede wells. Upper Dragon and Lower Dragon are the centipede's feelers; Big Sweet Water Well is its head; the wells in the eighteen villages of Fengtai are its legs. So what else can they be but centipede wells?"

And so this story has come down to us.

---

* After the establishment of the Republic in 1911, four more villages appeared there. Fengtai is now a district of Beijing comprising even more villages with wells not necessarily on the left of the temples.

The Cricket Cage Pedlar

EVERYONE knows Tian An Men in Beijing. Going into Tian An Men, passing through Duan Men, you go straight north to Wu Men, the Meridian Gate, the main entrance to the Forbidden City. The Forbidden City, with its brick walls behind which the Ming and Qing emperors lived and ruled, is now the Palace Museum. It has four gates north, south, east and west. But never mind the gates, let me just describe the watch-towers at the corners of the wall. Each of these four watch-towers in the Forbidden City has nine beams, eighteen pillars and seventy-two roof-ridges. Everyone who passes these magnificent towers exclaims, "However were those watch-towers built? Whoever can have designed them?" Well, there is a Beijing legend to answer these questions.

Beijing people say that after Prince Yan of Ming was enthroned* as Emperor Yongle in Nanjing, because he had lived in Beijing as a prince he decided to move the capital there and to send a trusted minister to repair his Beijing palace. He told this minister: On the outer wall of the palace, at the four corners of the Forbidden City, he wanted four magnificent watch-towers built. He warned him, "You're in charge of

---

* In 1402.

the construction. If you bungle it — off with your head!"

This imperial edict made the minister frantic. He had no idea how to build such watch-towers. He thought: Since these are the Emperor's orders, I'll have to build them for him. His words are our golden rules — there's no disputing them! I don't know how to set about this, but once I get to Beijing the builders there are bound to find a way.

As soon as this minister reached Beijing and had settled down in his hostel, he summoned all the overseers and master carpenters of eighty-one big contractors. He told them the Emperor's orders, and gave them three months in which to complete these four extraordinary watch-towers. "If you fail, of course the Emperor will cut off my head," he said. "But before that I'll behead the lot of you. So you'd better look out!"

The overseers and carpenters thought: Fine. Anyway, if we die so will you! But not one of them dared refuse. Not feeling sure that they could do this job, they kept getting together to work out a plan or tried to figure out something on their own. They complained, "There's no model for this extraordinary project, so how can we set about it? Where should the beams and pillars go? Where should the arches be put?" Some declared, "There's really no way we can start work." So they just had to rack their brains.

The time limit — three months — was very short. A month flashed past, and still the builders had not a clue as to how to tackle this work. They made many models, but none of them would do. By now it was the hot-

Watch-tower in the Forbidden City

test time of summer, the weather was stifling, and in their desperation they felt on tenterhooks.

One carpenter, too restless to stay in, went out to stroll through the town. In the distance he heard the chirruping of crickets and a pedlar's cry: "Buy my crickets! They will cheer you up when you can't sleep!" Going closer he saw an old man with two crates of cricket cages, large and small, all so skilfully made of millet stalks that they looked like towers and pavilions in a painting, and there were crickets in each. The carpenter thought: It's no use worrying; if we're done for we're done for. I may as well buy a pretty cage for fun. He asked the price and bought an ingeniously made, very dainty cage, which he carried back to the builders' living quarters.

At sight of it his mates bawled, "Here we are all

worried stiff, yet you bring in that rowdy cricket — what's the idea?"

The carpenter said, "To cheer you up when you can't sleep. Just look. . . ." He meant to go on, "See how cleverly the cage is made!" But just then he was struck by something special about it. He held up one hand, saying, "Don't make such a racket. Wait till I've done some counting. . . ." Then he carefully counted and recounted the beams, pillars and arches of the cricket cage, while the others watched intently in silence with bated breath. After finishing counting, the carpenter sprang up and slapped his thigh.

"See there — nine beams, eighteen pillars and seventy-two roof-ridges!" he cried.

That put fresh heart in them all. One by one they took the cage to count for themselves. "Yes, it really is a watch-tower with nine beams, eighteen pillars and seventy-two roof-ridges!" they said. From this cage they figured out the design of the watch-towers for the Forbidden City, made a papier-mâché model, and built the four towers still to be seen today.

Later, people said, "That old man selling cricket cages must have been a real Lu Ban!"* Ever since, whoever sees these four corner towers in the Forbidden City is bound to remember this story of the cricket cage pedlar.

---

* A legendary builder and craftsman, regarded as the patron saint of craftsmen.

Tian An Men's Stone Lions

BEIJING'S Tian An Men is a splendid monument, as everybody knows. This story is not about its history or structure, but only about the two stone lions on either side, south of Gold Water Bridge. Why have they a deep gash from a spear on their bellies? This means telling the story of how Li Zicheng, Prince Valiant, entered Beijing.

Prince Valiant led his peasant insurgent army out from Yan'an in Shaanxi. Wherever they went they stormed the Ming Dynasty's passes and cities as if splitting through bamboo, and on April the twenty-fifth, 1644, they finally reached Beijing. The night before, the last Emperor of Ming had hung himself on a locust tree on Coal Hill. All the high officials defending the city were "eunuchs", a useless lot. When Prince Valiant's troops fought their way to the city wall, the eunuch defending Guang An Men opened it immediately to welcome him in.

After entering Guang An Men, the prince rode over to Qian Men (Zheng Yang Men), having learned that the general defending it was Li Guozhen who had won a name in the Battle of Chessboard Street. Li Guozhen refused to open the gate and put up a fight to defend Beijing, but when he saw he was no match for the insurgents he abandoned his men and fled. What of his troops? Of course they opened the gate to welcome

Prince Valiant. He rode through Qian Men at the head of his men, passed Chessboard Street and entered the Da Ming Men.*

In the distance Prince Valiant saw a huge arch with five archways. His chief minister Niu Jinxing told him, "Look, Your Highness, there's the Cheng Tian Men.** It's from there the Ming Emperor issued all his imperial edicts to plague the common people."

Prince Valiant had long loathed the emperor of Ming. So on hearing this he snorted with rage, seized his iron backed bow and fitted to it an arrow with eagle feathers. He galloped towards the gate and, as soon as he was close enough to read the inscription Cheng Tian Men, he raised his bow, took aim and loosed off an arrow — whizz! — roaring at the same time:

"I'll teach you to support heaven!"

All this happened simultaneously, the twang of the bowstring and the prince's yell, and his shout was still ringing in the air when his arrow pierced the middle character "Heaven" on the gate. The insurgents raised a great cheer, while the government troops were stunned.

Next Prince Valiant slung his bow on his back and drew his spear with an iron shaft and steel tip. Everyone watched as, raising this spear, he spurred to the gate. South of it stood two ornamental columns and two marble lions, while north of it were two other marble

---

* The name was later changed to Da Qing Men and, after the establishment of the republic, to Zhonghua Men. Now pulled down, it used to stand south of the Monument to the People's Heroes.

** In 1651, its name was changed to Tian An Men, the Gate of Heavenly Peace. The original arch was torn down and the present structure built in its place.

Tian An Men

lions. We can pass over the ornamental columns; the four lions were fine marble statues. The two on the east have their right paw on a ball, their heads incline slightly east, but their eyes look west; the two on the west have their left paw on a cub, their heads incline slightly west but their eyes look east, as if intently watching the roadway between. Prince Valiant, his chief minister and generals were going up to have a better look at these lions, when suddenly a soldier shouted:

"Watch out, Your Highness! One of those lions just moved!"

"Rubbish!" roared Prince Valiant. "How can a stone lion move?"

In fact, he had noticed someone skulking behind one of the lions. Raising his spear he spurred to the lion on the east side and thrust at it. Dong! Sparks flew in all directions as he scored a gash on its belly. Then the man who had been hiding shot over to the lion on the west.

The soldiers shouted, "Watch out, Your Highness! An enemy!"

From under the lion's paw, Prince Valiant spotted a Ming general taking cover northwest of the lion. Pretending not to have seen him, he signalled to his generals, then speared the lion on the west. His generals meanwhile surrounded that lion and captured the Ming commander Li Guozhen. Since then both lions bear the imprint of a spear thrust.

So Prince Valiant took Beijing and the Ming Dynasty fell, and that is the end of our story.

Shi Cha Hai

SHI Cha Hai south of the Drum Tower in Beijing is a broad expanse of water surrounded by willows, locust trees and poplars — a lovely scene. You can boat there in summer and skate there in winter. After Liberation our government dredged the lake and set up a balustrade round it, making this ancient lake still lovelier. Beijing residents, when they talk fast, sometimes pronounce the *cha* in its name as *ji*, *jia* or *jiao* meaning vault and *shi* means ten. And that brings us to the story of the ten vaults of silver discovered by the Living God of Wealth Shen Wansan.*

All old residents of Beijing know of Shen Wansan, the Living God of Wealth. With a name like that he should have been very rich, but in fact he was penniless and had nothing but rags to wear. Then why was he called the Living God of Wealth? Because he could tell where gold and silver were buried. Why didn't he dig some up then to fit himself out? He couldn't. Normally he could only tell where there was gold or

---

* According to a Taoist, Shen Wansan is the deity in the Hall of the God of Wealth in White Cloud Monastery outside Xi Bian Men. Another tradition has it that Shen was a native of Suzhou at the end of the Yuan Dynasty, the richest man in the whole Yangzi Valley. When Zhu Yuanzhang became the First Emperor of Ming, he decided to build a wall around Nanjing, but as he was short of money Shen financed this. Later the Emperor, jealous of his wealth, had him executed. Shen never went to Beijing.

silver if people demanded some from him and beat him up; then in desperation he'd point somewhere at random and say if they dug there they'd surely find silver, maybe even gold. The harder he was beaten, the more caches of gold and silver he could locate. That accounted for his nickname the Living God of Wealth.

But who had the heart to beat him? His own family couldn't bring themselves to do it. As for ordinary people, they wouldn't beat anyone if they had no reason. So Shen Wansan and those who wouldn't beat him often went hungry and dressed shabbily.

One day the Emperor decided to build himself a northern capital. Not wanting to draw money from his treasury, he told his ministers to "raise funds locally".

His ministers objected, "It's impossible to raise such a huge sum from Bitter Sea Waste."

"Impossible or not, you must find some way!" said the Emperor.

Later someone told him about the Living God of Wealth and the Emperor, very pleased, ordered Shen Wansan to be brought to him at once. Armed with this "sacred edict", officers and soldiers rushed to Shen Wansan's house. When they reached his gate they laughed at finding the place so small and tumbledown.

A soldier said with a grin, "Fancy the Living God of Wealth living in such a hovel!"

An officer said, "Never mind what sort of place he lives in. Our task is to arrest him."

A soldier knocked at the gate. Out came an old man of medium height in a ragged jacket and pants.

"Who are you looking for?" he asked.

"Shen Wansan."

"I'm Shen Wansan," said the old man. "What can I do for you?"

"The Emperor sent us to fetch you," one officer told him. "Come with us."

Unable to refuse, Shen Wansan accompanied them to the palace.

The Emperor was in his audience hall when an officer came in to announce, "We have carried out your orders and brought Shen Wansan here — he is waiting outside."

"Bring him in."

When Shen Wansan went in and the Emperor saw him, he wondered: Can a poor old fellow like this be the Living God of Wealth? It didn't seem possible. But even if they'd nabbed the wrong man, he wouldn't let him go.

"Are you Shen Wansan?" he asked.

"Yes, that's my name."

"You know how to find gold and silver?"

"No, I don't."

"You don't know?"

"I don't know."

"If you can't find gold and silver, why are you called the Living God of Wealth?" fumed the Emperor.

"That's what people call me," said Shen. "But I'm no Living God of Wealth."

The Emperor lost his temper and pounded the table. "You've tricked people; you're a sorcerer!" He ordered his guards, "Take this sorcerer out and give him a good beating."

The guards dragged Shen Wansan off, pinned him down and started to beat him.

"Don't beat me!" he begged. "I'm not a sorcerer!"

"Then tell us where gold and silver are buried," they said.

"I don't *know* where there's any gold or silver!" he yelled.

"All right, then we'll beat you."

Thwack! Thwack! Thwack! They beat the poor man to a pulp, till he was streaming with blood. Then he groaned, "Don't beat me, I know where there's silver."

The guards stopped beating him and reported this to the Emperor.

The Emperor said, "Take him to dig it up. If there's no silver there, beat him again!"

Shen Wansan led some soldiers to an open space and pointing at it told them, "Dig here."

Sure enough they dug up ten vaults of silver. The story-tellers describe it in detail: ten vaults of silver with 480,000 taels in each, making 4,800,000 taels in all. Once this silver had been dug up it left a great pit, which later filled with water and was known as Shi Jiao Hai or Ten Vaults Lake.

After the city of Beijing was built, the Emperor, being insatiably greedy, wanted more gold and more silver. He had the Living God of Wealth hauled before him again. This time he glared at him even more viciously and bellowed to his guards, "Beat this sorcerer as hard as you can, till he produces nine vats of gold and eighteen vaults of silver."

Once again Shen Wansan was beaten nearly to death, till in desperation he led the soldiers out of An Ding Men and northwest to a stretch of empty land not far away.

He told them, "Under here are nine vats of gold and

eighteen vaults of silver, but you need a key to open them. What key? An aster. You must find one."

The soldiers were sure they could find an aster in that open stretch of land.

One officer ordered, "Look sharp and find an aster."

But strange to say, in all that open country there was not a single aster. Flying into a rage they roared at Shen Wansan, "Damned sorcerer, we should have killed you. You knew there were no asters here. Come on! We'll go back to the Emperor!"

When they dragged him back to the palace and reported what had happened, the Emperor was furious. He roared:

"Beat the sorcerer to death!"

Seeing how livid the Emperor was, his guards rained blows thick and fast on Shen Wansan, expecting him to disclose some other key with which to unlock the nine vats and eighteen vaults, to satisfy the Emperor. But Shen Wansan, being an old man, could not stand so many beatings. He gave a croak, his eyes rolled up and his legs stretched out rigid — the Living God of Wealth was dead! So they never found the key to the nine vats and eighteen vaults.

Later that place became the drill ground for the Imperial Army, but still no key was found there. Now big buildings stand there, but still no key has been found. However, right up to today, people tell how there were no asters on the drill ground to open up the the nine vats and eighteen vaults.

The Bell Goddess

BEFORE 1924, the people of Beijing and its northern suburbs every evening at seven o'clock would hear the continuous ding-dong of a bell — xie! xie! xie! — a most pleasing sound. Then, especially in the cold winter, mothers would tell their children, "Time for bed. They're striking the bell in the Bell Tower,* and the Bell Goddess wants her slipper.** Go to sleep now. Don't disturb the Bell Goddess." If children asked why the Bell Goddess wanted her slipper, their mothers would tell them this story.

Long ago, before the invention of clocks and watches, all provincial and county towns had drum towers. At seven in the evening, drums were sounded to let the citizens know the time. As Beijing was the capital, of course its drum tower had to be much higher and bigger than those in provincial and county towns, and a big bell tower had to be built as well to keep it company. So the Emperor issued an imperial edict and ordered the Minister of Works to build a great bell tower and cast a bell weighing ten tons.

The Minister of Works lost no time in summoning all the best foundrymen from the provinces to Beijing,

---

* The Bell Tower in Beijing, over ninety feet high and built entirely of brick, dates from 1272 in the Yuan Dynasty.

** The word for slipper is pronounced xie.

to discuss how to cast this great bell. When these skill-ed craftsmen were assembled, they talked the matter over and the Minister of Works put the best-known of them, Master Deng, in charge of all the rest. First they set up a large foundry west of the Bell Tower, and the workmen moved in to live there.

Master Deng was a family man with a wife and a lovely daughter, an intelligent girl who could read and write, and they were very comfortably off. They lived in an alley not far from the foundry, and when he went home in the evening they would laugh and chat to-gether without a care in the world.

Each time Master Deng came home, his daughter would ask, "Dad, has the bell been cast yet?"

"It soon will be," he told her, smiling. "Very soon."

Time slipped by, and when twenty days had passed the bell was finished — a big cast-iron bell. Master Deng reported this to the Minister of Works, who im-mediately informed the Emperor, requesting him to in-spect it. He was sure that after hearing the big bell the Emperor would reward him. The bell was set up and the Emperor arrived, but at sight of it his face darken-ed.

"Why not cast a bronze bell?" he demanded. "In-stead of this ugly black thing!"

When the bell was struck, the Emperor flew into a rage. "What sound is that?" he roared. "Those cracked notes won't even carry to my palace, let alone all over the city!" He penalized the Minister and warned him, "I give you three months, no more, to cast a ten-ton bronze bell. In fine weather its sound must carry to all four suburbs, and on windy days to forty *li* away. If you fail to make it, or botch it, I'll cut off your head!"

Then, with a swish of his sleeves, he stormed back to the palace.

The Minister of Works was frightened out of his wits. After the Emperor had left he bellowed at Master Deng, "Why lose face for me like this! I give you two months, no more, to cast the bell the Emperor wants. If you fail, or botch it, you'll be the first to lose your head. I won't spare one of the other workmen either!" This said, he got into his sedan-chair and left.

Master Deng and his mates were livid.

"He never told us he wanted a bronze bell!" one pointed out.

"He gave us iron not bronze!" another said.

They angrily took down the iron bell and left it lying on the ground, then discussed how to cast a bronze one. Master Deng went home fuming. At the sight of him his daughter asked, "Haven't you finished the bell, dad? Why are you angry?"

"Finished it?" Her father told her what had happened, making the girl angry too.

She could only say consolingly, "Well, you can think out a way to cast a bronze one."

Master Deng went on going to the foundry every morning and coming home in the evening. For the first six weeks or so all seemed to be well, but then a change came over him and he kept frowning and sighing. Questioned by his wife, he said nothing. Questioned by his daughter, he simply said, "It's all right." It dawned on the clever girl that her father was anxious because they had not succeeded in casting the bronze bell. Either molten bronze would not set, or it set in the wrong shape. For some time Master Deng had been off his food. His worried mates pulled long faces.

"We're really stumped," they said. "When the two months are up we'll be executed!"

When Deng's daughter knew this she was frantic too. Every single day she worried over her father, trying to comfort him when he came home and weeping with her mother when he was out. Soon the time would run out. The intelligent, lovely girl was at her wit's end.

Finally the deadline for casting the bell was reached. The day before, Master Deng had not gone home, making his wife and daughter fearfully anxious. So when she got up that morning, the girl told her mother she meant to go to the foundry.

"How can a girl like you go into the foundry?" her mother objected. When her daughter insisted she agreed, "All right then. But come straight home to set my mind at rest."

The girl changed into clean clothes and new embroidered slippers, then went to the foundry. The sun had just come out as she went in and found her dad and his mates milling round the great smelting cauldron, covered with sweat. In the sunshine their faces streaked with grime made them seem a horde of demons.

"It's me, dad!" she called.

Master Deng turned, and at sight of her his heart ached. He asked anxiously, "What are you doing here?"

"Because you didn't come home, mum told me to come and ask how you're getting on with the bell."

Before Deng could answer, one of the workmen put in, "The bell, eh! This bronze won't come right and today is the last day left. At sunset we'll all be dead men. Better hurry home, lass."

Hearing this, and looking at her dad and his mates, her heart bled for them. She thought: If dad and all these good uncles are to lose their lives because of a bell, I don't want to go on living. I'd rather die first! She gritted her teeth and braced herself to dash over to the great cauldron. Splash! She vaulted into it, spattering molten bronze in all directions.

When she darted forward the workmen had yelled, "Look out! Stop her!"

At first Deng had been stupefied. At this cry he charged after her, but too late to stop her. All he managed to catch hold of was one embroidered slipper. He held it, choking with sobs, for by now his daughter had become a wisp of blue smoke in the cauldron. Her father broke down, and the workmen all shed tears too, till suddenly one youngster shouted:

"Stop crying — look! The molten bronze has changed!"

The others crowded round to look and, sure enough, the molten bronze was giving off an extraordinary radiance. Sure now that they could cast it into a bell, they dried their eyes and set to work, and just as the sun was sinking in the west the new bronze bell, eight inches thick, was cast. So at last Master Deng and his mates had finished the task given them by the Emperor.

This new bronze bell was hung in the Bell Tower. Every evening at seven o'clock it is given eighteen swift strokes, then eighteen slow ones, then eighteen neither swift nor slow, and this sequence is repeated, making

Iron Bell

a hundred and eight strokes in all, each tailing off: xie! xie! xie!

Mothers hearing that sound say sadly, "The Bell Goddess is asking for her slipper again."

The foundry was dismantled, but that place is still called The Foundry, and there someone built a Temple of the Bell Goddess. Some say it was the Emperor who built it, others that it was Master Deng's mates, his daughter's uncles. But no matter who built that temple, the story of the Bell Goddess has been handed down. And what about the big iron bell?   That was left lying in The Foundry for hundreds of years, but in 1925 it was moved to the back of the Bell Tower and set up straight.   All who see it remember the story of the Bell Goddess.

Jiu Xian Qiao —
Liquor Immortal Bridge

IF you unfold a map of Beijing bus routes, in the northeast corner you will see a route through the suburbs which, starting from Dong Zhi Men runs eighteen *li* to Jiu Xian Qiao (Liquor Immortal Bridge), where used to be a little out-of-the-way village, and most people would probably never have heard of it if not for the legend about it. Now whole blocks of big buildings stand there, and it has a bus service and a sizeable market. For the sake of those who don't know the story of this place, let me seize this chance to record it.

Long, long ago someone led a river here. As there was a river there ought to be a bridge for the convenience of passers-by; and so a bridge was built, just when there's no knowing. The day that the bridge was finished, no one wanted to be the first to cross over it, for fear that his "bad luck" might clash with the bridge's "good fortune". So all waited on both banks for someone else to take the lead before they would venture across.

They waited till the sun was sinking westward, when in the distance they saw an old greybeard who was vigorously pushing a wheelbarrow. In the barrow were four liquor vats, two on each side. They watched the old man push his barrow straight to the bridge where, without any hesitation, he trundled it up to the top.

"What a sturdy old fellow he is!" they commented. "Those four liquor vats must weigh at least four hundred catties. Most likely he was born under a lucky star."

As the wheelbarrow reached the top of the bridge they exclaimed, "That takes strength!" Just at that moment, though, the barrow tilted to the right, two vats of liquor thudded on to the railing and plopped into the river.

"Too bad!" they cried. "Fish them out, quick!"

To their surprise Old Greybeard paid no attention, but swiftly pushed his barrow over the bridge and very soon vanished from sight. Everyone thought: How strange that he paid no attention when two of his vats fell into the river!

One shrewd fellow remarked, "Maybe he was an immortal. How else could he have pushed that barrow so fast, with a load of two hundred catties on one side and nothing on the other? You'd have expected him to move one vat over."

As they were discussing this, all of a sudden they smelt the aroma of liquor rising up from the river.

"Good liquor that!' cried one.

"Why not call this Liquor Immortal Bridge?" suggested another.

"Fine! Fine!"

So that is how the bridge got its name.

After that the villagers in the neighbourhood could always smell that aroma. Those who liked to drink took rice bowls from their homes to scoop up some water to taste. Ha! It really tasted like liquor, slightly diluted.

When word of this spread, the bank became a tavern where anyone could drink without spending a cent. People flocked there.

One day an old man with a black beard arrived, carrying a vat of liquor and some furniture. He set up a booth on the bank and began to sell liquor. On his booth he put up the sign "Genuine Vintage Spirits". After that, the river water tasted less of liquor every day, while the old man with the black beard did better business every day. The shrewd fellow thought this rather peculiar, and watching the old man carefully he grew even more suspicious. For Old Blackbeard sold liquor all day long, not closing his booth till dark. How many days would that vat of liquor last? Why had no one seen him go to replenish his supply? This shrewd fellow told his neighbours of his suspicions, and everybody started paying attention. In less than three days they discovered the trick Old Blackbeard was up to.

A village lad patrolled the river bank all night until dawn broke, but saw nothing out of the way. The next day, though, when the sun was high overhead, Old Blackbeard closed his booth, saying that he felt poorly, and that made the lad more suspicious. That evening, after an early supper, he squatted in a sorghum field just beside Old Blackbeard's booth to lie in wait. By midnight when all around was still, Old Blackbeard came out and standing on the river bank said to himself: "What a magnificent moon! If the hare in your Moon Palace drank my vintage spirits, it would have to smack its lips!"

The lad in the sorghum field knew that Blackbeard wanted to find out if there was anyone about. So he went on squatting there without a sound. Soon

Blackbeard went into his booth, to reappear presently
with a liquor vat and ladle. He walked down to the
river, glanced all around, then ladle by ladle filled his
vat with water and carried it back to his booth. Having
seen this monkey business with his own eyes, the lad
slipped home to think of a way with his neighbours to
settle scores with Blackbeard the next day.

The next day (this was the third day), the sun was
just veering south when the villagers of Liquor Immortal Bridge followed this lad to Blackbeard's liquor
booth. When they got there they found that he was not
alone: with him was Old Greybeard who had pushed
the wheelbarrow across the bridge, and another old
fellow with a snow-white beard over two feet long.
They were dismantling the booth and packing up. The
villagers were staggered.

The lad asked Old Greybeard, "Aren't you the
Liquor Immortal? A deity? What are you doing here?"

Old Greybeard smiled but said nothing.

Old Whitebeard roared with laughter. Pointing at
Greybeard he said, "This one who poured liquor into
the river is my son." Then pointing at Blackbeard he
said, "This one who waters down liquor is my grandson.
We're none of us deities."

While the villagers were struck dumb with amazement, Old Whitebeard directed his son and grandson
to carry off the liquor vat and furniture, and so they
left.

Since then the river water of Liquor Immortal Bridge
no longer tastes of liquor. And it is said that no pedlars
hereabouts dare water down their liquor, much less pour
liquor into the river, for fear of becoming Old Whitebeard's sons and grandsons.

Brimful Well

OUTSIDE An Ding Men in Beijing, at one side of Dong Tu Cheng (East Earth City) is a remarkable well: its shaft juts out of the ground and as it was always brimful it is generally called Brimful Well. Such wells are not too rare, but the fame of this one has spread far and wide. There are two reasons for this. The first is that towards the end of the Ming Dynasty, overfed officials with nothing to do wrote endless essays in praise of this well, and their readers assumed that it must be a really wonderful sight. The second is that a folk-tale grew up about it and was spread by word of mouth until all the common people, although they had not read the officials' essays, also knew about Brimful Well. We need pay no attention to the officials' essays; instead, let me tell you the folk-tale.

Why was Brimful Well always full? My old granny told me she had heard this story from *her* old granny. After Liu Bowen built Beijing in Bitter Sea Waste and Gao Liang raced for water, the city was short of water, and north of it was a stretch of arid wasteland. It was hard to get so much as a mouthful of water to drink — this was a real headache for everyone.

It occurred to them to sink wells, but they had no idea how to do this. They dug troughs, a cross between a ditch and a well, but when no water welled up they abandoned these. So no matter how many of these troughs they dug, they never struck water and grew more and more frantic. Some of them wept as they waited for Heaven to send rain. Each day as soon as it was light, they squatted outside on the ground waiting for rain, but they couldn't make it rain just by hoping!

One day, after the cocks had crowed three times, everyone gathered outside, but what could they say? They had nothing to talk about, they were too depressed. Just then they saw an old man with a black beard, who was striding towards them from the west, fulminating to himself. They didn't know what he was saying and wondered who could have provoked him so early in the morning.

A young chatterbox asked, "Who's provoked you, grandad, at your age?"

Before Old Blackbeard could answer, an elderly man nudged the youngster and said with a sigh, "Here we are all worried to death! Why ask him who has provoked him?"

In astonishment Old Blackbeard inquired, "Brother, why have you all gathered here to worry together?"

The elderly man smiled at the idea of gathering together to worry. He stood up and answered, "You're from far away, elder brother, so you don't know our problems." He explained that they had no water to drink and hadn't succeeded in sinking wells, ending up, "How can we help worrying, brother?"

Old Blackbeard burst out laughing. "Don't stay squatting there, folk," he said. "Stand up and listen to me." Everyone sprang up to hear what he had to say.

"Do you good folk know who provoked me?" he asked.

"No, do tell us," they said.

"It was my elder brother. For generations our family have lived by sinking wells for other people. We heard that far, far to the east, over a thousand *li* from here is a district plagued by drought, so we're on our way to sink wells for the people there. Last night we put up in a temple to the west, and I proposed turning in early, so as to get up early and set off in the cool of the morning. But the Taoist in that temple loves to play chess, and my elder brother is crazy about chess too; so they played all night, and when I woke this morning they were still hard at it. So I left in disgust."

The villagers did not care who had annoyed Old Blackbeard, but they were pleased to hear that he could sink wells. They begged him to help them, and he agreed readily, saying, "If I hadn't been prepared to sink wells for you, I wouldn't have told you how my brother provoked me. Just show me these wells you've dug, to see why you haven't struck water."

The villagers stopped worrying as they led Old Blackbeard to look at all their wells.

He told them with a smile, "There's underground water everywhere here; you just don't know how to dig. You have to stick to your guns. Three more shovels, and these wells of yours will strike water. Fetch me a shovel, quick!"

A youngster who was a good sprinter flew off to fetch a shovel. Old Blackbeard taking it sized up the situation and dug up two shovelfuls of earth, one on the left side and one on the right of a dry trough they had abandoned. The soil turned dark as water seeped into it, a sight to rejoice all eyes. Then the villagers saw Old Blackbeard stoop to shovel with all his might into the middle. As soon as he shovelled up the soil this third time, water came spouting out.

"Water! What a great water spout!" they cried, jumping for joy.

Old Blackbeard had jumped out of the well. Now he stood beside it to watch. Very soon water brimmed up to the mouth, very soon it flooded out, and very soon a big river was flowing through the plain. The villagers, with no experience of wells, did not know what was happening. They saw Old Blackbeard stamp in exasperation, saw him break out in a sweat.

"Confound it!" he swore. "I've dug through the sea vent!"

The villagers were staggered. While they were at a loss and Old Blackbeard was frantic, they heard a shout some distance away to the west:

"A pretty mess you've made of things, Number Two!"

They all looked westwards and saw a white-bearded old man with something on his back, who came flying towards them. When he drew nearer they could see that it was a cauldron he had on his back. Old Whitebeard came up to the well. Without a word he glared at Old Blackbeard, then took the cauldron, turned it upside down and flung it into the well. Strange to say, at once the water stopped gushing out, just leaving the well brimming with crystal-clear water.

Old Whitebeard told the villagers, "You've water to drink now, folk. This well will always brim with water." He scolded Old Blackbeard, "Number Two, you're so hasty, you nearly caused a flood. I told you to wait till I'd finished my game of chess, but you were too impatient. What if you'd swamped this place?"

"Didn't you say we'd still over a thousand *li* to go?"

Old Whitebeard told him with a smile, "I said it was far yet near."

Then, chatting and laughing together, the two old brothers went off.

Since then Beijing has had this Brimful Well. Its bottom is not flat but convex, and people say that is the big cauldron which Old Whitebeard threw down it.

The Stone Statues
at the Ming Tombs

SINCE Liberation a big reservoir has been built near the Ming Tombs, about which there are various tales. All visitors there know that the avenue leading in from the front archway is lined with statues. There are twenty-four stone animals: four lions, four griffins, four camels, four elephants, four unicorns and four horses. There are also twelve stone men: four military officials, four civilian officials and four statesmen of noble rank. But all these magnificent statues are slightly chipped or damaged. How could such hard marble be chipped? The local people have a story about this.

Emperor Qian Long,* so they say, wanted to set off his grave by moving the statues from the Ming Tombs there. He told his Prime Minister, Hunchback Liu, his plan. Hunchback Liu thought: If he moves those statues away, won't that spoil the Ming Tombs? But of course he had to obey the Emperor. He said, "Good! Good! Quite right, Your Majesty."

So the Emperor sent his Prime Minister to the Ming

---

* Tradition has it that Qian Long (1736-1796) took the great pillars from the halls of the two tombs Yong Ling and Ding Ling, substituting inferior timber, and then wanted to move the stone statues.

The Stone Statues at the Ming Tombs

Tombs to reconnoitre and figure out how best to move the statues. After putting up in the state hostel, Hunchback Liu went to have a look at them. The more he looked the more beautiful he found them, and the more convinced he was that they shouldn't be moved, but he could think of no way to keep them there. Like an actor in a play, he proclaimed the imperial edict to the statues:

"Listen and obey, stone figures and stone beasts!" he cried. "An imperial edict gives you three days in which to move away. Do you agree to this?"

The stone figures said nothing, the stone animals kept still. Hunchback Liu turned to tell his attendants, "The statues haven't said a word or moved. That means they are willing."

His attendants suppressed smiles and expressed agreement. Then he led them back to the hostel.

That night, at midnight, the Prime Minister was sitting up racking his brains for a way to keep the statues at the Ming Tombs. Suddenly he heard a commotion outside, as if many people had come. He opened the door to look. Ha! There stood the twelve stone figures from the Ming Tombs.

"You should be preparing to move," he said. "Why come here to disturb me?"

The four noble statesmen in front replied, "We have come to beg Your Excellency's help. This has been our home for hundreds of years, so we really don't want to leave. Do let us stay here intact, Your Excellency!"

That word "intact" gave Hunchback Liu an idea. He fumed, "What insolence! How dare you stone statues flout an imperial edict? So you want to stay here intact and save your hides? I have no patience with you!"

He sprang up and struck one statesman's cheek. Why should Hunchback Liu spring up? For one thing, those statues are taller than real men; for another, the Prime Minister was a hunchback. Besides, when the stone statesmen heard him say "So you want to stay here intact and save your hides", they had nodded as if they understood. And when he raised his hand to strike them, instead of dodging they smiled. In a twinkling the four statesmen's faces were mutilated or their robes were torn, yet they still looked very pleased. The four military officials and four civilian officials submitted equally cheerfully to a beating, knowing there was a reason for it; so none of them hit back. After all twelve statues had been mutilated, the statesmen said, "Thank you, Your Excellency. Excuse us for disturbing you. We'll go back now." And off they went at the head of the four military officials and four civilian officials, leaving the Prime Minister there in the hostel.

The stone statesmen went up to the stone animals and bellowed at them, "You twenty-four beasts are still sitting pretty here, disgusting creatures! Draw your swords, commanders, and slash each of these brutes!"

"Very good!" cried the four military officials. And, though not knowing the reason, they carried out their orders, wounding all twenty-four stone animals.

The next morning the Prime Minister deliberately told his attendants, "The Ming Tombs are deserted, yet there was such a row last night that I couldn't sleep properly."

His attendants replied, "We didn't hear anything."

That set Hunchback Liu's mind at rest, since they knew nothing of the trick he had played. He told them, "Well, let's go and have another look at those stone figures and stone animals, before going back to report to the Emperor."

When they reached the statues, Hunchback Liu made a show of inspecting them carefully, one by one.

"Look!" he exclaimed suddenly. "They're all mutilated! How can they be used for our Emperor? They aren't fit for his use!"

His attendants saw that the stone figures and animals were indeed mutilated. They all agreed, "Our Emperor can't use these."

And afterwards? Hunchback Liu went back to report to the Emperor: The stone figures and stone animals at the Ming Tombs were all chipped and damaged, not fit to be used. And so those statues remained at the Ming Tombs. People going there today still tell this story.

Black Dragon Lake

A beauty spot northwest of Beijing is called Black Dragon Lake.* Everyone knows of this lake, but few except the local people know of White Dragon Lake to its north. Are there dragons in these lakes? No. It's because there are no dragons in these Dragon Lakes that the folk-tale which I shall now tell you has been handed down.

You've already heard the story of how Gao Liang raced for water. That described how Gao Liang overtook the Dragon King with his wife, son and daughter at the foot of Jade Spring Hill, and speared Dragon Girl. At once Mother Dragon flew away, carrying her daughter to Black Dragon Lake. Then what became of them? That is our story today.

When Mother Dragon had carried her wounded daughter to Black Dragon Lake, she plunged below a rock and hid there, nursing her daughter. Before long, Dragon Girl's wound healed. Mother and daughter made their home under that rock in the lake. Dragon Girl liked to play about. When she was tired of staying at home she would swim in the lake; when she was tired of swimming, she told her mother she wanted

---

* Black Dragon Lake, northwest of the Summer Palace, is now a sanatorium.

to take the form of a pretty girl and go ashore to have some fun.

Her mother had misgivings and warned her, "Don't wander too far away or stay too long. You don't know these parts — take care no one pesters you."

Dragon Girl agreed to this. Every day she went ashore for a romp, and as no harm came of this she gradually stopped worrying. One day she was picking wild flowers on a hillside when all of a sudden a young man appeared beside her. Dressed all in white, with a dragon design on his hat, he looked very vicious.

Before Dragon Girl could say anything, he asked, "Know who I am, little girl?"

Being the granddaughter of the old Dragon King and the daughter of the new Dragon King, she naturally knew a dragon when she saw one. She told him, "You are White Dragon."

White Dragon roared with laughter. "His Royal Highness, mind you! Do you know to whom that lake you live in belongs?"

"How can a lake belong to anyone?"

"It was granted me by the Emperor," said White Dragon. "That lake's mine, you can't live there."

"I don't know what you're talking about," retorted Dragon Girl, pouting. "It belongs to whoever lives there."

"You insist on staying put?"

"Yes!"

"All right then," White Dragon sniggered. "Go and tell your mother you'll have to live with me and be my concubine."

Dragon Girl turned livid with anger. "You brute!" she swore. "Don't talk nonsense! We'll stay put, and see what you can do about it!" Swishing her green jade earrings, she darted back to the lake.

White Dragon called after her, "Hey! Stop, dragon slave girl! Tell your old Mother Dragon that I live in White Dragon Lake to the north. I give you three days and then, if I get no answer, I'll take your mother on and we'll see who wins!" With that he left.

Dragon Girl went back to the lake and burst into tears. When her mother asked the reason, she described her whole encounter with White Dragon. Mother Dragon was furious. She told her daughter:

"It's the fault of your grandad who tried to drown all the people in Beijing, and your dad who tried to take away their water so that they would die of thirst. Now they'll never see the light of day again — that serves them right! That's left just the two of us, and this vicious dragon cub wants to bully us. Well, I'll fight him to the finish!"

"Can you beat him, mum?" asked Dragon Girl.

"I doubt it," said Mother Dragon. "For one thing, he's on home ground here. For another, he has people to supply him with food. But I'm not afraid of him."

It was true that White Dragon had people to give him food. Knowing that Mother Dragon and Dragon Girl would not do as he wanted, he turned himself into a warrior dressed all in white and went into the village. He announced to the villagers, "I am the Dragon King." Then he pointed at Dragon King Temple on the bank of White Dragon Lake. "That's where I live. Three days from now I shall have a trial of strength with a savage dragon in Black Dragon Lake. You'll see two water-spouts in the air, one black, one white, and the white one will be me. If you see the white water-spout dwindle, lose no time in throwing steamed buns into White Dragon Lake. Once I've won the fight I'll see to it that you have good weather for your crops. If I lose, don't blame me if you all get drowned in a flood!"

For fear, the villagers had to agree to this.

To go back to Mother Dragon. She knew that White Dragon would frighten the villagers into supplying him with food. What about her? She called together all the fish, large and small, in Black Dragon Lake.

"I meant to settle down here as your neighbour," she told them. "But now that odious dragon in White Dragon Lake has challenged me to a battle. I have no provisions for fighting — what's to be done? I shall have to feed up for this battle on you, my friends. If I win, of course I shall bring you back to life. If I lose, my daughter will do it."

In face of a dragon, the fish dared raise no objection. And now Mother Dragon took the form of a great black dragon scores of feet long and, opening her huge jaws, swallowed up the fish, large and small, one after the other.

On the third day there came a tremendous clap of thunder out of the blue, and a bright white water-spout flew up from White Dragon Lake. It shot to Black Dragon Lake, but before it reached there a jet-black water-spout flew up from that lake. The two water-spouts grappled together in mid air for three days and three nights. Several times the white spout dwindled, probably because of exhaustion, but then it soared up again, probably because steamed buns had been given to it. However, the black water-spout never dwindled.

In the third evening, with a thunderous splash, both water-spouts subsided into the lake, leaving two dead

Black Dragon Lake

dragons on the hillside; for White Dragon and Mother Dragon, their strength spent, had died of exhaustion together.

Dragon Girl was heart-broken after her mother's

death, and remembered her promise to the fish to restore them all, big and small, to life. With a stamp of
one foot she hurtled against the rock in the lake, smash-
ing herself into smithereens which scattered in the water
and changed into remarkable little fish. These fish have
wide tails, long dorsal and pelvic fins and four little
pectoral fins. Something special about them is that in
the sunlight they shimmer like a rainbow, and people
say these colours come from Dragon Girl's embroidered
gown. They have two small jade-green gills, said to be
Dragon Girl's green jade earrings. They usually hide
under the rock in the lake, as Dragon Girl was told to
by Mother Dragon, not venturing up to the surface. They
can strike their heads against stones. If kept in a fish
tub with pebbles on the bottom, they may knock into
the pebbles and set them clinking, and then people say
Dragon Girl is thinking of her mother. These fish are
known as Bu fish.

After the death of White Dragon, Mother Dragon
and Dragon Girl there were no more dragons here.
Only the two lakes are left, one called White Dragon
Lake, the other Black Dragon Lake.

The Flower Goddess

NOT far from the Western Hills, east of Sleeping Buddha Temple, is the Hill of Ten Thousand Flowers. On it stands the little Temple of the Flower Goddess. The local people put great faith in this goddess. According to them, no one knows how many years ago or from how far away a pretty girl of fifteen or sixteen came here and slipped into this little temple to sit on the altar in front of its deity's statue. Then, closing her eyes, she turned into an immortal. When the local people discovered her transformation, it caused a great stir and they set to work to refurbish the temple for her. To please the goddess, one family vowed to plant a flower on the hillside; others vowed to plant ten flowers or a hundred flowers; and so as time went by this became known as the Hill of Ten Thousand Flowers, and she as the Flower Goddess.

Little girls hearing this story want to get to the bottom of it and ask their old grannies, "Where did the goddess come from? Why did she choose this temple in which to become an immortal?"

Their grannies shake their heads and say, "That's something I can't tell you. When my granny told me this story, she said I wasn't to pass it on."

"Well, I won't pass it on either. Do tell me, there's a dear granny!"

"All right, but you mustn't tell a soul. If you do, the

Flower Goddess will be angry and won't watch over us."

Then the grannies tell the little girls the story. And when the little girls become grannies themselves they tell their own grandchildren — how else could this story have come down to us?

So this is the story of the Flower Goddess. In a village separated from this by one hill then another, one stream then another, lived a wealthy landlord who had an only daughter. Of course she was her parents' darling. What name did they give her? She had no name, but they called her Darling. When she was one or two, she was so sweet that her father and mother loved her even more dearly and called her "our precious Dar'ing". When she was five or six, Darling's cheeks were as red as apples and she was even more adorable; but unluckily, the year that she was six, her mother who had doted on her died.

Being motherless was bad enough, but what upset Darling most was that her father married again, and her stepmother was a terror! After three years this stepmother gave birth to a daughter too, whom they called Pet — of course a child with a mother is bound to be petted. Darling loved her little sister, but her stepmother seeing this said, "Don't put on that act in front of me. My Pet doesn't want you to love her."

At mealtimes, Darling was afraid to take second helpings of rice or side-dishes, but urged her little sister to eat more. Then her stepmother scolded, "You hateful brat, do you want to stuff Pet to death?"

Whatever Darling did, her stepmother found fault. And her father called her stupid, making her very wretched. Worse still, he stopped loving her.

When Darling was twelve, her stepmother and father told her, "You're too big to be idling at home, not earning your keep. Go out and herd the cattle with the cowherd."

So every day after that Darling went out with the cowherd.

Little girls hearing this story ask their grannies, "Who was the cowherd? How did he come to be working for their family?"

The grannies answer, "Nobody knows his name. All that's known is that his dad owed the landlord money, and when he couldn't pay up the landlord was angry, so he took his little son in lieu of payment, and from the age of seven the boy herded their cows. Over the years there's no knowing how often the landlord beat him or made him go hungry. Darling pitied the cowherd and often smuggled him some left-over food; and he pitied Darling too, and often picked wild flowers for her to play with. Herding the cattle together they became good friends, and the cowherd plaited wreaths of flowers for Darling while she patched his clothes for him — they were very fond of each other. There was nothing wrong with that, but it annoyed Darling's stepmother. One day she told her husband, "The cowherd's already fourteen. Don't let him play with Darling."

"Why, have you seen them misbehaving?" the landlord asked in dismay.

The stepmother pretended to be reluctant to speak out. She faltered, "Well, no, actually I haven't. But if we wait till people see them, won't it look bad?"

The landlord suspected the worst of everyone — how else could he have made such pots of money? A few days later the cowherd disappeared, sold to another rich landlord far away. Darling naturally missed him. As time went by she learned that her father had sold him to a family far, far away. She thought: My stepmother doesn't love me, and neither does dad. They have my little sister to keep them from feeling bored; so I may as well leave. No matter how many hills and streams lie between, I must find that unlucky cowherd. One night she slipped out of the back gate and ran away.

Small girls hearing this ask, "Didn't that rich landlord look for Darling?"

Their grannies answer, "Never mind about that."

"Did Darling find the cowherd?"

"She crossed one hill then another, one stream then another, walking ten whole days and eight nights without seeing a sign of the cowherd. Finally she reached this Hill of Ten Thousand Flowers of ours. She was too hungry, too tired, to go any farther; so she sat down on the altar to rest her feet and, all of a sudden, changed into an immortal."

After finishing this story, grannies warn little girls, "The Flower Goddess doesn't like to hear any mention of stepmothers, and she also hates to hear any mention of cowherds. So be careful what you say when you go to her temple!"

Swallow Terrace

TRADITION has it that one of the eight sights of Daxing County is the terrace where in autumn swallows muster. That is a well-known place, and the local people tell a tragic story to explain why "swallows muster to cry over autumn". In the southeast of the little town of Caiyu in Daxing stands an earthen terrace over twenty feet high, the Terrace Where Swallows Muster. Every autumn swallows are said to assemble here before leaving Beijing to winter in Hainan Island, and here they cry for two days before flying south together, crying over autumn. Do they flock here every year? Well, of course no one has seen that. So let's say no more about this, but get on with our story.

Once upon a time, long, long ago, in a village not far from the Terrace Where Swallows Muster, there lived a rich old landlord. How much land did he own? No one knows. All we know is that he had a large estate and an only daughter, Ruby, a pretty, intelligent child. The old landlord and his old wife doted on her: she was really the apple of their eye. Ruby had never learned to read, for how many girls in those days were able to study? Like other children of her age she liked to play and enjoyed picking wild flowers, plaiting little flower baskets, catching dragonflies or crickets.

What made her happiest of all was that she had a friend Little Swallow. The son of Old Yu in the east end of the village, he was a bright, handy boy; and he too was the apple of his parents' eye. Old Yu was poor. He and his wife had only two *mu* of land to till, enough to feed them, not enough to clothe them; so every day Little Swallow gathered firewood or dug up herbs to help his dad and mum to make ends meet. In the fields, Ruby met Little Swallow out digging up herbs. They were seven or eight then, so they quickly became the best of friends. She helped him look for herbs, and was so clever that she knew which could be eaten fresh, which dried to be eaten in winter. Little Swallow also helped her pick wild flowers and make flower baskets, but Ruby always said, "Brother Swallow, let me help you find herbs instead to eat." They were most attached to each other. But when the old landlord discovered this he was displeased.

"You must stop playing with that pauper's brat, Ruby," he said. "We don't want his poverty to rub off on you."

Ruby had no idea what he meant, and went on playing as before with Little Swallow.

The years passed till both children were twelve or thirteen. After playing together for five or six years they were closer friends than ever. The old landlord refused to put up with this. He told his wife:

"Our Ruby's a big girl now. She mustn't fool about with the son of that beggarly Yu."

"Quite right!" agreed his wife. "After all, our daughter's a young lady. No young lady of her age should gad about outside. From now on we'll keep her indoors."

So Ruby became a young lady forbidden to leave the house. Still Brother Swallow was always in her thoughts, and he missed her all the time too. Sometimes she climbed up the rockery in their garden to watch him pass outside the wall; and then she would call out affectionately to him. But the time was always too short, and besides there was that hateful wall between them.

During the next two years Ruby learned embroidery. Strange to say, the flowers she embroidered were never as lifelike as the swallows she loved to embroider. Each time she embroidered a swallow she tossed it over the wall to Brother Swallow, making him very happy. She had given him ninety-nine embroidered swallows, and this day she had just finished the hundredth one. When she examined it, why, it looked more spirited than the other ninety-nine.

She said to herself, "This time Brother Swallow is going to be extra pleased. If only this swallow could fly and sing!"

As she said this, she heard a cheep, and the embroidered swallow flew out of the window crying, "Brother Swallow! Quick, hide yourself!"

Ruby was stunned. She wondered: How can an embroidered swallow fly? Why should it want Brother Swallow to hide? She couldn't guess the reason. And that swallow, after flying out of her window, flew straight to the eaves of Old Yu's cottage, still crying, "Brother Swallow! Quick, hide yourself!" This stunned Old Yu and his son. They couldn't guess either why the swallow was calling out this warning.

That same evening the blow came. Ruby's father had seen her give her friend all those embroidered swallows, and he thought it a disgrace to their family. Not wanting the news to get out, he sold a hundred *mu* of good land to bribe the magistrate to have Swallow sent far,

far away. That magistrate had no principles at all. Having accepted the bribe he did as the landlord wanted and, having no conscience, sent men to Yu's cottage to arrest young Swallow. Regardless of the facts of the case, he found Swallow guilty of "being in league with bandits", and banished him to Hainan Island in the south. Old Yu and his wife knew their son was innocent, and Swallow knew this was unjust, but in those days the poor had nowhere to turn when they were wronged.

After Ruby's hundredth embroidered swallow flew off, she was on tenterhooks, wondering what was happening to Brother Swallow. Every day she climbed up the rockery, but she never saw him go past and felt filled with foreboding.

One day she was going to pay her respects to her parents when, outside the window, she heard her father say, "Now the Yu family's young bastard has been banished to Hainan Island, he can never come back."

"We must hurry up and arrange a marriage for Ruby," her mother said, "before there's any more trouble."

When Ruby heard that, her ears buzzed. This was like a bolt from the blue. Instead of going in to see her parents she went back to her room. She knew Brother Swallow couldn't be guilty of any crime, this was all her parents' doing; but she had no way to rescue him. She fell ill and kept to her bed. The landlord jeered, "Serves her right." His wife called in doctors to examine her, but they informed her that Ruby was not ill. Her mother was rather upset, while her father simply laughed.

After Ruby fell ill she still longed for Brother

Swallow's return. From spring till autumn she longed, but there was no word of his coming back. Then one day a swallow alighted under the eaves, crying, "Brother Swallow's dead and gone! Brother Swallow's dead and gone!" The bird cried most plaintively, as if shedding tears.

In a panic Ruby asked, "Little swallow, is my Brother Swallow dead?"

"Dead and gone, dead and gone!" repeated the swallow.

"If he's really dead," said Ruby, "please circle our eaves three times."

The swallow flew round in three circles. Then Ruby fainted and the bird flew away.

Ruby wept and cried, shedding tears of blood, and that same night she died. When the landlord and his wife knew this, of course they quarrelled.

The landlord said, "Serves Ruby right."

Where did they bury her? They dug her grave south of the village, and as time went by the grave-mound became over twenty feet high. On that earthen terrace grows a strange kind of grass called Swallow Grass. The juice squeezed out of its blades is a red dye with which women can dye cotton red or rouge their lips; so it is also called Rouge Grass. It grew out of swallows' blood. Every autumn, before flying off to Hainan Island, the swallows first asemble on Ruby's grave and there they sing for two days, asking her if she wants any message taken to Brother Swallow.

Urn Hill

PICTURESQUE Longevity Hill and Kunming Lake in Beijing's Summer Palace are known throughout China, known through all the world. They received their names from the emperors and empress dowagers of the Qing Dynasty. Before that, before the Summer Palace was walled off and monopolized by the imperial house, Longevity Hill was known as Urn Hill, and Kunming Lake as Dabo Lake. Many families lived at the foot of the hill on the bank of the lake. Some grew paddy, some grew other crops or fished; for the place was not then an imperial pleasure ground with halls and pavilions. This story is not about the history or sights of the Summer Palace, nor about the height of Longevity Hill or the depth of Kunming Lake. It tells why Longevity Hill used to be called Urn Hill.

Many years ago, an old fellow named Wang Laoshi lived there and worked as a hired hand for a rich landlord. He was so honest that the villagers all called him Honest Wang. Honest Wang lived northwest of Urn Hill, but worked southeast of it. Every day he crossed Green Dragon Bridge to make his way south of the hill and north of the lake to the landlord's estate. He had done this every day since his twenties, year in year out for more than thirty years, working steadily for the landlord all that time.

This year Honest Wang would be sixty. He thought to himself: I've worked all my life but have nothing to show for it, no money and not a single son or daughter. For thirty years and more I've walked past this hill; I should leave something on it to be remembered by. He decided that on his birthday he would plant a pine on the hill.

Some days later it was Honest Wang's birthday, and with a chortle he told his wife, "We're poor with no son, no daughter and no money. I'm going to plant an evergreen pine on the hill, so that folk will have something to remember us by. That's how Honest Wang will celebrate his sixtieth birthday!"

His wife gave a humph then said, "There's something in that — it'll be a poor man's treat."

Honest Wang shouldered a shovel and tucked under one arm the pine sapling he had ready, then off he strode over Green Dragon Bridge to the southeast foot of the hill, where he often stopped to rest. Having put down the sapling, he found a place where there were no rocks to plant it, then shovelled down over a foot till he suddenly heard a clank. Confound it, he thought. I've struck rock. How can I plant a tree here? After shovelling out more earth he took a look and saw a slab of stone covering a porcelain urn. When he removed the stone, he saw to his amazement that this urn was a treasure-trove, full of gold, silver and jewels. He took them out and spread them all over the ground.

Honest Wang thought uneasily: What use are all these precious stones to me? They might land me in big trouble! He decided not to take the urn away, but put back the precious stones one by one, covered the urn with the stone and buried it again. The pine sapling he planted to the east of the urn. With a smile he said to it, "Hurry up and grow, little sapling. When you're a big tree, folk will come and rest in your shade." Then he shouldered his shovel and left.

Once home, Honest Wang described to his wife how he had dug up an urn full of precious stones and then buried it again.

"You did right," said his wife. "What use would such things be to the likes of us? They'd be bound to land us in trouble. You did quite right."

Then both of them laughed, and that was how Honest Wang celebrated his sixtieth birthday.

Honest Wang still went every day to work for the rich landlord, and each time he passed in front of Urn Hill he watered the pine sapling. It grew so green and verdant that the sight of it warmed his heart. And as time went by he forgot about the urn full of precious stones.

One day when the hired hands and casual labourers had knocked off at noon, the landlord came to the threshing-ground wearing a straw hat to keep off the sun to see if they were sleeping or not. He was pleased to find them seated beneath a tree chatting, because that meant they would not oversleep and go back late to the fields. As he came over to exchange a few words with them, one of the casual labourers spotted a pearl on his hat.

"That's quite a size, that pearl on your hat, boss," he said.

The landlord curled his lip. "You louts can't have

seen one this size before," he boasted. "This is a very precious jewel."

The others agreed they had never seen such a large pearl. Only Honest Wang burst out laughing.

"I have!" he said. "I've seen plenty bigger than this."

The other men asked Honest Wang where he had seen them and he described how he had dug up an urn full of precious stones, then buried it in the same place in the ground. They called him a fool for letting slip such a chance to make a fortune.

The landlord rolled his eyes, cleared his throat and said with a scowl, "Mind what you say! That's the treasure buried by my ancestors to keep control of the hill. Since it has been found, we can't leave it buried there. Come along with me to dig it up."

The hired hands and casual labourers knew that the landlord was lying, but they had to go with him as, being rich, he had the upper hand. Honest Wang led the way, and the rest took picks, shovels, rope and a carrying pole, while the landlord kept an eagle eye on them as they hurried to Urn Hill. There Honest Wang pointed out where the urn was buried.

"Be careful how you dig," the landlord ordered. "Can't have you damaging my family urn. And when you've dug it up put it on the ground. I want to open my family treasure myself."

Not daring to object, they shovelled down a foot or more to the stone slab, at the sight of which the landlord beamed. Then digging around it they dug up a big porcelain urn more than three feet high, which they stood on the ground. The landlord gloated over this beautiful celadon urn.

The Summer Palace

"See there, you lot," he said. "This is the 'treasure to keep down the hill' buried here by my ancestors. Wait till I open it — it'll be an eye-opener for you."

With a great show of reverence the landlord stepped forward to remove the stone cover. The inside of the urn was too dark for him to see anything there, so he groped in it with his hand, and felt something soft and squirming. As soon as he withdrew his hand, out slithered some great snakes which coiled tightly around him. Then out flew a horde of scorpions and centipedes, which bit and stung him so that before he could utter a sound he was stung to death. Then what did everyone do? Well, they carried him back, and his son mourned for him. As the landlord's death was due to his own greed, no one else could be blamed for it.

What about those snakes, scorpions and centipedes? They had slithered or scuttled away.

The next time Honest Wang passed the foot of Urn Hill, the pine sapling was still a verdant green and the big porcelain urn was still standing on the ground. Honest Wang said with a sigh, "Let's leave you here, empty urn, to 'keep down the hill'." So he buried the urn again in the same place, then went home. That is how this hill came to be called Urn Hill.

Iron Screen Wall

ON the north bank of Bei Hai, northeast of Five Dragons Pavilion, stands a most unusual screen wall: rust-coloured and apparently made of iron. It is called Iron Screen Wall. In fact it is not made of iron but of pumicite-stone, which just happens to look like iron. This Iron Screen Wall used not to be in Bei Hai; it was moved there in 1946 from Fruit Market Street inside De Sheng Men. To begin with it did not stand inside De Sheng Men either. Over five hundred years ago it stood in front of a temple outside that gate. Why was it moved to Fruit Market Street? A folk-tale tells us the reason.

This is another story about dragons. Most of the dragons in Beijing folklore are terrifying and set on destroying the people of Beijing; but the dragons in this story of Iron Screen Wall are kind-hearted. You have heard a good many stories about terrifying dragons, so now let me tell you about these kind-hearted ones.

Long, long ago two dragons, husband and wife, lived in Bitter Sea Waste. Having no desire to destroy Beijing, after the city wall was built they turned into an old man and an old woman and, lying low, led a quiet life. After the completion of the city wall, the remarkable thing was that a violent northwest wind used to blow for three or four days without any let-up, and this happened over and over again, each time smothering Beijing in inches of dust. This worried the old man and his wife. They said, "If this wind keeps up, Beijing will be buried in dust."

The old woman said, "I suspect some monkey business."

"So do I," agreed the old man. "But I can't put my finger on it."

The two cf them brooded over this for some days, but could not think what to do.

How about that wind? It really was extraordinarily violent. One day an old man was riding a long-eared donkey to Qian Men when suddenly this northwest wind sprang up and whirled the donkey sky-high. It pricked up its ears in fright, and the old man riding it shut his eyes; but presently the wind died down, the donkey landed on the ground, and the old man opened his eyes. Why, they were outside Cong Wen Men — they'd flown three or four *li* through the air! Another day, an acolyte in Imperial Aunt's Temple in the western hills was playing in front of the temple when this great wind sprang up and whirled him sky-high. He was so terrified, he buried his head in his arms and shut his eyes, his heart going pit-a-pat. He thought: I'll be smashed to death for sure! But presently the wind died down and he landed on the ground. When he opened his eyes he found himself in Beijing — he had flown thirty to forty *li* through the air!

There was really something uncanny about that wind. Hearing of the strange way the donkey, its rider and the acolyte had been whirled through the air, the two dragons, now an old man and his wife, felt even more disturbed.

One day the old man suggested, "Let's go for a stroll and see if we can't get to the bottom of this."

His wife agreed, "Exactly what I was thinking. Just sitting at home we can't find out who's up to this monkey business."

So they went out. Which way did they go? The wind blew from the northwest, didn't it? So they made their way northwest. Wherever they went, they saw only people buying or selling things or carrying loads, quite ordinary people, discussing ordinary affairs and going about their ordinary business. They saw nobody and nothing at all suspicious. They went on northwards till they came to the northwest part of the wall.

The old woman grumbled, "You don't use your head, just go where your feet carry you, and here we've reached the wall without finding a thing. We'd better have a look outside."

The old man chuckled, "Don't worry. If we turn east we can go out of the north gate."

They went eastward skirting the wall, and saw a strange sight. You are bound to want to know: "What strange sight did that old man and his wife, the two dragons, see? Hurry up and tell us." But here I must make a digression. That old city built in the Yuan Dynasty is now known as the Earthen City. In Yuan times that north gate east of its northwest district was known as Jian De Men.

Well, to get back to our story. What strange sight did the old man and his wife see? They saw two people seated at the foot of the wall: an old woman in her fifties, and a boy of fifteen or sixteen. Both wore dun-coloured clothes, and their clothes and faces were covered with dust — they were an obnoxious sight.

And what do you think they were holding? Each had a dun-coloured sack. The old woman was stuffing hers with sand, the boy his with cotton-wool. They were talking together, but all that the dragons could hear was, "We'll bury their Beijing in dust — just see if we don't!"

The old man and his wife, the two dragons, looked at each other, and the old woman nodded. They knew that the woman in her fifties must be a wind witch, the boy must be a cloud spreader. And here they were plotting to bury Beijing in sand! Just then Wind Witch and Cloud Boy raised their heads and saw them. At once they sprang to their feet.

"Time to go home, grandson," said Wind Witch. "We don't want your mum to start worrying."

Old Man Dragon knew that they meant to run away. He sprang up to Wind Witch, and his wife barred Cloud Boy's way. The old man wagged his finger at Wind Witch and bellowed, "What are you up to? Why should you bury Beijing and all the people living here in sand?"

Wind Witch snickered, "How dare you question our great scheme, old fellow? If they could build Beijing to get in our way, then we can bury their city!"

The old man roared with laughter. "Don't you dare do such a wicked thing, old crone!" he cried. "Hurry up and give me that ragged sandbag of yours." Then he pointed at Cloud Boy. "And you leave your sack of mouldy cotton-wool here. You're too young to be learning bad ways."

Before Wind Witch could answer, Cloud Boy made haste to empty his sack. As black clouds billowed out of it he yelled, "Let out your wind and sand, grandma, quick!"

The old man and his wife, the two dragons, opened their mouths together and sucked those turbid black clouds into their bellies. All this happened in a flash. And just as the b!ack clouds were swallowed up, Wind Witch loosed swirling sand to choke the old man and his wife. Atishoo! Atishoo! They both sneezed. Fine! With those sneezes of theirs out gushed four jets of clear water which swept towards Wind Witch and Cloud Boy. With a howl of dismay Wind Witch caught hold of Cloud Boy and flew up into the air. The old man and his wife changed back into dragons and chased the two of them north.

After that there were fewer sandstorms in Beijing, and everybody said that was because Old Dragon and his wife had chased Wind Witch and Cloud Boy away.

Iron Screen Wall

As those monsters were afraid of these two dragons, people decided to make an iron screen wall with a dragon on each side, so that Wind Witch and Cloud Boy would never dare come back. That is how this handsome Iron Screen Wall was made.*

Some years later the north side of the city wall was torn down, and Beijing was extended southwards. What had been the north part of the city lay waste again, and once more the people of Beijing were plagued by sandstorms. They were desperate but could think of no way out.

An old man, wise in the ways of the world, suggested, "This must be because Iron Screen Wall is too far from the city for Old Dragon and his wife to control Wind Witch and Cloud Boy. We must find some way to cope."

Those who knew the story of Iron Screen Wall agreed with the old man, but didn't know what to do.

Then a clever fellow stepped forward. "Don't worry," he told them. "I have an idea."

What was his bright idea? To move Iron Screen Wall back into the city. Everyone thought that a really clever idea, and so they moved the screen wall to the Fruit Market inside De Sheng Men, setting it up in front of a temple there. Later that street was called Iron Screen Wall Alley.

Well, that is the end of this story. Do you want to know if Iron Screen Wall, once it was moved back to the city, really kept out the wind and sand? The answer to that is: No!

---

* In fact, the designs on the screen wall are unicorns, not dragons. However, their scales resemble those of dragons.

The Motherwort in the Temple of Heaven

ALL the buildings making up the Temple of Heaven* can be called world-famous. Who hasn't heard of the Hall of Prayer for Good Harvests, the Imperial Vault of Heaven, the Circular Mound and the Echo Wall? A reproduction of the Temple of Heaven is used as the trademark of many goods. But we needn't dwell here on the architecture of the Temple of Heaven. Instead let me tell you about a strange herb that grows here. Its young shoots, rather like asparagus, are known as dragonbeard rushes. When this plant ripens, its stalks and leaves provide effective medicine for women's diseases, and this is called motherwort medicine. Why does so much motherwort grow in the Temple of Heaven? There is a folk-tale about this.

The story-tellers say: Before the Temple of Heaven was built or this district incorporated into the city, there was a stretch of open country here where peasants scraped a living from the soil. One family here was called Zhang. The father had died over two years before leaving his old wife with no son but only a daughter of sixteen or seventeen. With no man in the

---

* The Temple of Heaven was built in 1420. Motherwort still grows there, and up to the end of the Qing Dynasty shops there sold herbal medicine made from it.

house and no money, they lived from hand to mouth.
The old mother, missing her husband and worried because they had no one to till the land, fell into a decline
and her illness went from bad to worse day by day. This
made her very worried, her daughter even more so. They
consulted doctors, who prescribed all kinds of medicine,
but none did her any good. Just after the harvest that
autumn, the daughter decided to go to the northern hills
to find some efficacious herbs, because when she was
a child her parents had told her that deep in the northern hills grew plenty of magic herbs which would cure
any illness, no matter how serious. So now she told her
mother that she was going to the northern hills.

Her mother said anxiously, "How can a girl like you
go all that way!"

"Don't worry, mum," said her daughter. "I'll be
very careful." She asked an old woman who lived next
door to look after her mother for her; then taking some
food for the journey she set out to the northern hills to
find magic herbs.

Once out of the gate Little Zhang had no idea which
way to go. She decided: The northern hills must be to
the north, so I'll head in that direction. After walking
for a whole day, she saw some hills. She went on for another three days, but still she hadn't reached the northern hills, although they looked closer and closer. One
day she came to a pass. She was wondering whether to
go through it or not when she saw a white-bearded old
man come out of it.

He asked her with a smile, "What brings you deep
into the hills all on your own, lass?"

She told him she had come to look for herbs to cure

Temple of Heaven

her mother's illness. Then she asked, "Are there magic herbs in these hills, grandad?"

"Yes, there are."

"How can I find them, grandad?"

With a smile Whitebeard pointed towards the hills. "Climb these hills, lass, take seven turns to the left and eight turns to the right; when you're hungry eat pine kernels, when you're thirsty drink spring water bright; and when you see heaven on earth you'll find magic herbs all right."

He reeled this off like a jingle, and she found the directions clear except for that bit about heaven on earth; but before she could ask him to explain, the old man was already some distance from the pass. Then Little Zhang climbed the hill, took seven turns to the left and eight to the right, picked up some big pine kernels to stay her hunger, lapped up some bright spring water to quench her thirst, and when she was tired slept in a hollow in the hillside. On awaking she went on climbing.

How many days it took her I forget, but one day she reached the summit of a hill. There was a pool there of translucent water reflecting all the wisps of cloud in the sky. She was staring blankly at it when she heard girls' voices behind her. Looking round she saw two young girls approaching her, one in a snow-white costume, the other in yellow silk embroidered with white plum-blossom. They were both quite ravishing.

As they drew near, the girl in white asked with a smile, "What are you staring at, big sister? Don't you recognize this 'heaven on earth' of ours?"

At this mention of "heaven on earth" Little Zhang was delighted. She asked, "Do you sisters have any magic medicine? Do give me some to save my mother's life!"

The girl in yellow said, "You don't need to explain, big sister. Grandad Whitebeard has told us all about it. I've a bag here of potent medicine. When you go home and brew it, it will set your mother right." With that she handed her a little bag.

The girl in white said, "In this bag of mine are some seeds of the herb. Once your mother's better, you can sow them, and when they've grown they'll cure other women who have the same illness."

The girl in yellow urged her, "Go home quickly, big sister. We won't see you off. Just remember White Sister's advice!"

Having thanked them from the bottom of her heart, Little Zhang started downhill. After a little way she turned her head, wanting to have a last look at these two kind girls, but there was no sign of them. All she saw was a white cockatoo and a fallow-deer, flying and racing west from "heaven on earth".

Strange to say, it had taken Little Zhang seven days and eight nights to reach the hill, yet she returned home in no time. There she brewed the medicine and gave it to her mother, who in a few days recovered, to the great delight of her daughter and their neighbours. Then Little Zhang scattered the seeds all around their house, and in spring they sprouted green and lush, in summer they flowered, and in autumn they seeded, increasing from year to year. Women who fell ill could be cured by brewing medicine the way Little Zhang prescribed. What did they call this herb? Everyone said, "Good-hearted Little Zhang found this efficacious herb to cure her mother, so let's call it motherwort." And so the name motherwort was handed down.

Some years after that, Beijing became an imperial city, and one Emperor decided to pray to Heaven for protection and to build a Temple of Heaven in this place where motherwort grew. When the Temple of Heaven was finished, its courtyards were still overgrown with motherwort.

The Emperor fumed, "We can't have all these weeds in my Temple of Heaven. Uproot them all, quick!"

It so happened that the mother and the wife of one of his ministers were just taking the medicine made from motherwort. So he told the Emperor, "Your Majesty, these aren't weeds, they're a vegetable called dragonbeard. Aren't you a dragon, Your Majesty? If you have them all uprooted, your imperial beard won't grow."

As the Emperor wanted to grow a beard, he left the motherwort in the Temple of Heaven. Since then its young shoots have been called dragonbeards.

Lushi and His Dragon Disciples

AMONG the sights of Beijing are the well-known Eight Great Sights of the western hills over thirty *li* from the city. Going there makes a pleasant outing. In fine weather in spring and autumn, you see many parties of primary-school, high-school and college students flocking there to admire the Eight Great Sights of our beautiful capital. It is not difficult to get there by bus, or you can take a train to Green Shade Hill, Flat Slope Hill or the Four Terraces at the foot of Lushi Hill. From there you can stroll up to see the Eight Great Sights: the Temple of Lasting Peace, the Temple of Divine Light, the Three Hills Monastery, the Temple of Great Sorrow, Dragon King Hall, Fragrant Boundary Temple and Precious Pearl Cave — that's seven sights, isn't it? And if you climb another hill after turning north from the Four Terraces, you find yourself on Lushi Hill where stands the Attaining Buddhahood Temple. To its west is a sheer cliff, and the temple has no pillars, its east and north sides abutting on the hills which overhang it. Mimo Precipice here is even better known than the temple. For years it has been said that this precipice was where the founder of the Mimo sect, the monk Lushi, lived and took Big Blue and Little Blue as his disciples. All visitors to the Eight Great Sights talk about this, so let me tell you the story.

The story-tellers say: Over 1,360 years ago, at the end of the Sui Dynasty, the empire was in such a turmoil that the monk Lushi who lived south of the Changjiang River (Yangzi) decided it was impossible to stay there; he would rather roam the country. But where should he go? No one else knew of a good place, and he had no idea either. He thought: I'll take a small boat to the north. When it's taken me several thousand *li* and can't go any farther, I shall stop there.

He went to the river bank to hire a boat. Asked where he wanted to go, he told the boatmen his plan.

The boatmen laughed and said, "North of the Yangzi is land; north of that is the Yellow River; and north of the Yellow River is more land. How can our boats take you there?"

Lushi did not lose heart, but walked along the bank every day making inquiries. One day he came to a small inlet and saw a little boat hidden among the rushes, with only two youngsters aboard, their hair combed into tufts, each wearing a suit of blue cotton. The elder seemed less than twenty, the younger only fifteen or sixteen.

Lushi asked, "Do you take passengers?"

"We do," said the elder. "Where do you want to go, holy father?"

Lushi told them his idea, whereupon the two brothers looked at each other and smiled. "We'll gladly take you," they told him.

"What are your names?" asked Lushi.

The elder said, "As we like to wear blue, I'm called Big Blue and my brother Little Blue. We have no home, so we live here in the river."

When they had agreed upon the fare, Lushi stepped

aboard and Big Blue and Little Blue manned the oars, one on each side. And so they set off north. How they left the Yangzi I have no idea, nor how they reached the Yellow River and left it again. On and on they went north-north-west. Lushi asked no questions about this course, and neither brother offered an explanation. In less than two days they reached a great ravine with ranges of hills to its west, a precipice to the east and a dead end to the north — to the south was the way they had come. The boat could go no farther.

Lushi said, "Set me ashore at the foot of that eastern precipice."

But the precipice was too high for him to climb up from the ravine. Before he could say another word, the water in the ravine rose suddenly, carrying the boat up with it till they were level with the top of the cliff. Then the three of them stepped ashore. At once the water subsided, the boat sinking down with it. Lushi did not ask how the water had risen or subsided, neither did Big Blue or Little Blue explain this. When they questioned the local people, Lushi was staggered: These were the western hills west of Bitter Waste, two or three thousand *li* from their starting-point! And they had come all that way in only two days. But again he asked no questions, and the brothers offered him no explanation.

Big Blue and Little Blue said, "Holy father, our boat has been wrecked, so we can't go back south of the Yangzi. We'd like to become your disciples."

Lushi told them, "I didn't want to stay in the south for fear of the turmoil of fighting; but you were born and raised there, why don't you want to go back?"

Big Blue answered, "Our home there is under the

River Master's control, and he ordered us to use our boat to drown people. When we refused to do this, he threatened to kill us. That's why we came here to take refuge with you."

Lushi did not ask who their River Master was, and neither did Big Blue or Little Blue tell him. So he accepted the brothers as his disciples.

Below the cliff he hollowed out Lushi Cave, where he lived with his two disciples. They got up early each morning to sweep the floor, cut firewood and prepare meals for their master. The rest of the time they bathed in the deep lake down below while Lushi devoted himself to chanting the scriptures, not asking what they were up to, and Big Blue and Little Blue never told him either.

Day after day went by. One year then another passed. The third year there was a bad drought. The fiery sun scorched the earth and shrivelled the leaves on the trees, making everyone very anxious, Lushi too. He sat at the mouth of his cave beating a wooden fish to pray for rain. Then along came Big Blue and Little Blue, laughing and chatting as they brought a bucket of water up from down below.

Lushi snapped at them in annoyance, "What are you laughing at? Such a bad drought, yet the two of you are still grinning!"

Big Blue said with a smile, "Never mind the drought. We can make rain!"

With that he raised the bucket and flung the water up into the air. That dazzling sheet of water, blown by a cool breeze, changed into a black cloud, and Big Blue and Little Blue bounded straight into it.

"Mercy!" shouted Lushi.

For instead of Big Blue and Little Blue he saw two blue dragons with bared fangs and outstretched claws shoot into the cloud and vanish. Then it poured with rain for three whole days and nights. On the third day Big Blue and Little Blue came back, but instead of returning to Lushi Cave they hid themselves in the deep lake, never to appear again.

Later, in which year there's no knowing, people said: If Lushi was able to have blue dragons as his disciples, he must be the founder of his Mimo sect. So they called that cliff Mimo Precipice. And whenever there was a drought, the peasants who depended on the weather would come to beg Big Blue and Little Blue to make rain. But according to the old folk, the very old folk, the dragons never granted their request. So Mimo Precipice became one of the Eight Great Sights of the western hills.

Topsyturvy Temple

IF you take a bus or trolley out of Fu Cheng Men, get off at the first stop, the west end of Fu Street, and go up the north slope, that will bring you to Ci Hui Si (the old Temple of Compassion and Wisdom). People may not know it by that name, but if you ask for Topsyturvy Temple* even little children can show you the way there. Why is it called Topsyturvy Temple? Well, there is something peculiar about its main hall which has puzzled people for years. The main hall faces south and naturally has a front door and a statue of Buddha inside; and behind that statue is a four-leaf door facing north. It's this door that is peculiar. In it is a little round hole, and anyone approaching from outside casts his reflection through the door; but the peculiar thing is that the reflection of those going west appears to be going east, and vice versa. And these images are all upside down. Even the reflection of the trees in the back courtyard are upside down. Everyone marvels over this, and so a folk-tale has spread.

It is said that before this temple was built, to its north was a place called Hall of Tranquil Bliss or Palace Attendants' Slope, a graveyard for palace attendants. Palace attendants were, of course, ladies-in-waiting. In the old days emperors had the whole empire ransacked

* Built in 1592.

for pretty girls to be sent to the palace to wait on the "Son of Heaven." This was described euphemistically as "the selection of exemplary maidens". Once in the palace they were never allowed out again, never able to see their families again, so what girl wanted to be shut up in the palace? What girl didn't long to go and visit her parents? But there was nothing they could do about it.

As time went by some girls fell ill, some died and were buried in Palace Attendants' Slope. So many died that it dawned on one Emperor: These ladies-in-waiting don't like living in the palace. I must find some way to make them realize their inferiority and their unlucky fate, so that they will be happy to serve as attendants. He told his Prime Minister in confidence what was on his mind, and ordered him to find some way to solve this problem. The Prime Minister later hit on a solution and had this temple built south of Palace Attendants' Slope. The small hole in the temple's back door was said to have been made by an immortal to reveal people's "fate."

After that, when a lady-in-waiting died, the Empress would put on a show of grief and tell the others, "Too bad! Such a good girl she was, but she wasn't born lucky enough to wait on the Emperor. You were all as close as sisters, so I'll give you a day off to see her to her grave, though, mind you, this is against the rules of our imperial household."

After being shut up in the palace for so many years, of course all the ladies-in-waiting longed for an outing. After an old maid had taken them to see the dead lady buried in Palace Attendants' Slope, she told them, "Now you can amuse yourselves." Pointing to the temple to the south she said, "When you've had your fun, we'll go and drink tea in that temple."

Those ladies-in-waiting who for years had never seen the countryside, never seen wild flowers or the western hills, really felt at home there and feasted their eyes on everything around. After enjoying themselves like this for a while they went in to look at the temple and have some tea.

"I forgot," the old maid in charge told them. "There's a relic here of an immortal. Why not have a look at that."

"We'd like to see it," said the ladies-in-waiting.

The old maid divided them into two groups, one to stay in the hall, one to go outside. Those in the hall exclaimed, "How is it they're all upside down? And though they're walking west they all seem to be going east."

The old maid smiled but said nothing until they had finished watching. Then with a stern look she told them solemnly, "You saw that. You're all of you ill-fated, inferior creatures, that's why your reflections are upside down. So accept your fate and see to it that you serve the Emperor faithfully."

The ladies-in-waiting didn't know what "fate" meant. They let the old maid lead them all back to the palace.

After that, the Emperor went on abducting the common people's daughters every year, and every year some of them died broken-hearted because they were so badly treated. When finally no more ladies-in-waiting were buried in Palace Attendants' Slope, this temple really became a historical relic.

The Tired Pagoda

DUE east of the Temple of Heaven in Beijing, southeast of the Stadium and north of Dragon Pool Lake there used to be a big seven-storeyed octagonal pagoda a hundred feet high. This splendid pagoda stood in the back yard of the Scriptures Repository Temple built in the Jin Dynasty. That temple fell into ruins long ago, leaving only the Tired Pagoda.* And thereby hangs a tale. Travellers passing Fengtai on their way to Beijing by train pass this place, and if there is an old Beijing resident in the carriage he may tell the other passengers the story of the Tired Pagoda.

The hub of Beijing is naturally the gate of Tian An Men. East of this axis is the East City, and west of it is the West City. Strange to say, the East City has not a single pagoda, while the West City boasts the Two Pagodas Temple (now pulled down to widen the road), the Pagoda of Ten Thousand Pines, the White Dagoba in White Dagoba Temple, and the small white dagoba in Beihai Park. People living in the West City gloat, "The West City has five pagodas, the East City none!"

Kindly Old Lu Ban, on a visit to Beijing, was very put out to find no pagodas in the East City.

---

* The Chinese characters *fa* in Scriptures Repository Temple (Fazang Temple) and Tired Pagoda (Fa Pagoda) are homophones. This pagoda collapsed in 1971.

He said to his younger sister, "Little sister, what a fine capital Beijing is. It's too bad all the pagodas are concentrated in the West City. That rather vexes me."

His sister said, "If that vexes you, big brother, it's easily remedied. Why don't we give the East City a handsome pagoda?"

"Fine," said Lu Ban. "Let's tour the country to find a good model." So the two of them sailed off on a cloud on their search.

One day they reached the West Lake in Hangzhou and saw Thunder Peak Pagoda.

"What a handsome pagoda, brother!" exclaimed Lu Ban's sister.

"Let's make one like this," he answered.

With the two of them working at it, the job was soon done. They sat on the bank of the West Lake from sunset till the first watch*, by which time a splendid seven-storeyed octagonal pagoda was completed.

Lu Ban's sister told the pagoda, "Worthy pagoda, there's no pagoda in the East City of Beijing. Would you like to go and live there?"

The pagoda droned, "Yes, I would."

"Off you go, then!" said Lu Ban. "But mind you don't stop to rest on the way. Set out during the second watch and you'll be in Beijing by the fourth. You must find yourself a site before the fifth**, because after that you won't be able to move — no, never again!"

---

* About 7 p.m.
** The second watch was from 9 to 11 p.m., the fourth from 1 to 3 a.m., the fifth from 3 to 5 a.m.

The Tired Pagoda

The pagoda agreed to this. It promptly changed into a swarthy old man with a pointed head, dressed in a grey cotton gown. Having taken his leave of Lu Ban and his sister he turned to the north and whizzed off, disappearing from sight.

Sure enough, in less than two watches he had covered several thousand *li* and was approaching Beijing before the fourth watch. When he reached the back of a

big temple (the Scriptures Repository Temple) he heard
laughter and voices in the courtyard and craned his
neck to look over the wall. Some monks on night duty
were gambling at the foot of the wall. He thought: I've
been travelling half the night and come thousands of
li. Now I'm fagged out. There's not much farther to
go, so I'll rest here and have a bit of fun watching them
gamble. So from outside the wall he watched intently,
unable to tear himself away. He watched game after
game, until finally one player beat all the others. The
winner laughed heartily while the losers cursed their
bad luck, and he found this so diverting that he boom-
ed, "Fine!"

The monks looked round at this bolt from the blue
and saw a huge swarthy fellow taller than the wall. Not
stopping to pick up their money, they rushed into the
temple. Just then the morning bell sounded from the
temple's bell-tower, and in the distance cocks crowed.
The big swarthy fellow could not move another step.
With a roar he turned back again into a handsome
seven-storeyed octagonal pagoda, reaching a hundred
feet into the air. Then — crash! — squeezed out by the
pagoda, the temple's back wall collapsed.

The abbot came out with his acolytes, all of whom
were struck dumb at sight of this great pagoda.

The abbot urged, "Hurry up and kowtow with me to
this precious pagoda! It's a gift to us from Heaven."

As soon as they had knelt down some monks cried,
"Look, Master Abbot, look! Where did all these coins
on the ground come from?"

Those monks who had been gambling were out of
luck. None dared say: That's our money. At the sight

of it the abbot said with a smile, "This must have come with the precious pagoda. We can build a wall with it."

So a wall was built enclosing the pagoda. Now both temple and wall have gone, but the pagoda still stands by the roadside. Beijing people say, "This pagoda built by Old Lu Ban stopped here because it was tired from travelling. Let's call it the Tired Pagoda."

Discriminating Bell Temple

THE outer wall of Beijing has three south gates, that on the east being Zuo An Men (Left Peace Gate). Are there any stories about the district outside it? My old granny told me not a few, some long, some short, and I remember several. Let me first tell you one of these. Less than three or four *li* southeast of Zuo An Men is a place called Fen Zhong Si (Discriminating Bell Temple). Here is its story.

How did Discriminating Bell Temple come to be given that name? My old granny told me: Once upon a time there was a strange bell in that temple, which could of course be heard in all the villages around. Strangely enough, that bell sounded different to different people. Stranger still, it sounded not like a bell but like a word in each one's ear. My granny never heard or saw that bell, she just heard the accounts passed down from one generation to the next. It was said that to a layabout that bell sounded like "Get up! Get up!" To someone hard-working it sounded like "Take it easy!" To a shepherd boy it sounded like "Graze your sheep!" In spring it sounded like "Clean out the barn!" At the time of the wheat harvest like "Thresh the grain!"

How could one bell make so many different sounds? Old folk handed down the story that in this village there was once a kindly old fellow with no means of support, who lived all on his own. The other villagers asked him to be their watchman and he agreed.

"What wages do you want, grandad, for sounding the night watches for us?" they asked.

"I don't want any wages," he told them with a smile. "Save up the money you would have given me till there's enough to cast a bell. Then the bell can replace my clapper."

The other villagers agreed. And the old man started sounding the watches each night.

He took his job very seriously, that old watchman, and as time went by came to know all the villagers inside out. When he sounded the fifth watch he discriminated between them. Passing the gate of a young fellow whom he knew to be hard-working, he struck his clapper gently to let him know that there was no hurry to get dressed. Passing the gate of a young layabout, he struck his clapper so hard that it seemed to be made of iron, not wood; and although the young fellow cursed him for his pains he would get up and go off to work.

The old watchman sounded his clapper for many years, stopping only when the new bell had been cast. Hadn't he said that the bell could replace his clapper? And so it did. But that bell was just as strange and just as "provoking" as the old man, sounding different to different people. So they called it a discriminating bell, and the temple was known as Discriminating Bell Temple.

The Black Monkey

ANYONE going in the old days outside Qian Men in Beijing to Fresh Fish Mart, a bustling street opposite Da Shan La was bound to marvel at the black lacquer monkeys with flashing golden eyes displayed in front of all the hat shops there. Why was this? Some people said: That's the shop-sign for hatters. Others said: That's not a black monkey but a monster which eats wild beasts of every kind. No one knows that monster's name, but there is a folk-tale to explain how it became a hatters' sign.

Towards the end of the Ming or at the start of the Qing, near the foot of the western hills stood the home of an old hunter. He spent his whole life hunting, yet still his family lived from hand to mouth. After the old hunter died, his son, not yet twenty, became a hunter too and went out every day in search of game to provide for his mother. But although he went out every day he never bagged any good game, and this made him worried. So one day he told his mother that he was going deep into the mountains to hunt.

"You mustn't do that!" she told him frantically. "Your dad never went so far, not in all his years as a hunter!"

"Don't worry, ma," he answered. "I'm quick on my feet, and I'll be very careful. I can't come to any harm."

When his mother had given her consent, he got ready

his hunting tackle and provisions for a few days, took leave of her and set off into the mountains.

The young hunter struck into the mountains, crossed range after range of hills, valley after valley, yet to his dismay still caught nothing but wolves and hares. One day he came to a mountain higher than any he had ever seen, its peaks rising sheer to the sky, with a long pass leading straight through it. He thought: There's bound to be fine game here: I must catch some to please ma.

Just then he heard a rushing wind from the pass, and saw a cloud of dust rise there. He knew that a great pack of wild beasts was coming, so to keep out of their way he found a sturdy tree with thick foliage, shinned up it and hid himself in its forked branches to wait there quietly. No sooner had he hidden himself than the beasts came rushing out, crying in distress. Since he had hunted with his father since boyhood, he knew that these beasts were being chased by some more vicious creature. He immediately fitted an arrow to his bow. The next second up they all came: tigers, leopards, deer, red-eyed monkeys, grey wolves and black foxes! There were beasts of every kind. What could this mean? And when this great pack of animals reached the tree where he had hidden, they all knelt down below it, crying out pitifully, to his great astonishment.

A black fox acting as their spokesman pleaded, "Take pity on us, sir, and save us! A monster whose name we don't know has come to the mountain. It looks something like a monkey, with glittering golden eyes and jet black fur. A real terror it is. It's eaten two lions, a tiger and three leopards! And it's after us now. Please save us, kind young man."

The young hunter wondered: What can this monster

be? Will I be able to catch it? Although he had doubts he answered confidently, "Run off quick! I won't let it get you!"

With a shout of joy the animals bolted off. After they had gone, he fitted a poisoned arrow to his bow, and in a flash a black creature came flying out of the pass. It looked much like a monkey, but its fur was as black as ink, bright and glossy as velvet. The young hunter thought: This is an intriguing creature. If I can kill it, that's bound to bring me good fortune.

The black creature drew near, staring at the tree as if aware that someone was hidden there, and its golden eyes flashed and sparkled. Before it had come to a halt, the young hunter let fly an arrow — whizz! He was a crack shot; that arrow pierced the black creature's brain, making it leap up with pain; then after thrashing about on the ground it flopped dead. The young hunter watched it lying there for a while before he ventured to climb down the tree. When he went over to look closer and stroke its fur, he was very pleased: What beautifully soft fur! He skinned his prize, left the mountain and started back. When he told his mother at home of his adventures, she marvelled too and wondered what this creature was.

A day later the young hunter announced that he meant to go to Beijing to sell this fur.

His mother's advice was, "Don't sell it to anyone who doesn't know good furs. Poor though we are, if you meet someone understanding, even if you get a lower price you'll be able to find out what the creature's called."

"Right you are, ma," said the young hunter.

He flung the black fur over his shoulders and went

Qian Men

into Beijing. Once there he called on several furriers, but at sight of his fur they all of them shook their heads.

"Fancy bringing us a black monkey skin!" sneered one.

"This small black monkey can eat lions?" another cried. "Catching lice is more in its line!"

"How can a fox talk?" another challenged. "What rubbish!"

All these taunts annoyed the young hunter, but what could he do? He left the furriers and roamed the streets, just following his nose till he heard a sudden shout:

"Hey, young fellow, is that fur of yours for sale?"

"Yes, it is." He looked up and saw a white-bearded old man, beaming with smiles at the sight of the fur.

The old man asked, "How did you come by this fur?"

"I caught it."

The old man gave a start. "Caught it? Tell me quickly how."

The young hunter described his trip into the mountains, then asked, "Do you know what this creature is called?"

The old man nodded. "You pulled off a tough job, youngster. This is a most vicious beast. If he so much as sees your shadow, you're done for! Few people know his name, which is Ink Monkey."

"You're an expert, grandad," the young hunter said. "Will you buy it?"

"I can't afford to," said the old man. "But I'll find you a good customer." He took the youngster to a big official's home, and there they sold the Ink Monkey's fur for a high price. After pocketing this sum, the young hunter was naturally very pleased. He asked the old man, "Grandad, why should that fur fetch such a high price?"

"Ah, you don't understand. Ink Monkeys are treasures. A hat made from that fur is impervious to snow or rain."

"Well, that big official must have pots of money."

The old man smiled. "No, this is an investment. He'll give this Ink Monkey fur to some bigger official or even to the Emperor, to secure his own position and help him win promotion."

The young hunter could not understand this, could only assent. Later, on the old man's advice, he learned from him how to make hats, then used this money he had made to set up as a hatter in Fresh Fish Mart. His hat business did so well that his mother no longer worried about food or clothing; and because he owed this to that Ink Monkey, he made an Ink Monkey of wood and had it lacquered black to put up as his shop-sign. The passers-by did not know this was an Ink Monkey; they just called it the Black Monkey. As time went by, other hatters in Fresh Fish Mart all hung up Black Monkey signs too; so there is no saying which of all those hat shops belongs to the descendants of the young hunter.

The Stone Monkeys
on Broken Rainbow Bridge

EAST of Wu Ying Dian (Hall of Martial Valour) in the Forbidden City is a bridge with a beautifully carved stone balustrade, called Broken Rainbow Bridge. On each stone pillar of the balustrade squats a stone monkey (in fact they are lions, but in this tale they are monkeys). One of these monkeys has a ladle in its left paw, while with its right it is hitching up its skirt. None seeing it but marvel at the skill of this spirited carving.

One old eunuch said, "Each time the imperial equipage passed this way, a yellow cloth cover was slipped over this stone creature. Why? So as not to let its uncouth appearance alarm the Emperor."

Another said, "No, that wasn't the reason. It was because one Emperor lost his temper over something and kicked one of his own sons to death in front of this stone. Later on he felt so remorseful that each time he passed here he grieved and to spare him that his attendants prepared a yellow cloth cover to drape over this stone, thinking: out of sight, out of mind."

Both eunuchs were right, but now let us hear a folk-tale which tells quite a different story.

In a certain reign of one dynasty, the old Emperor in the Forbidden City had a favourite concubine, who

used to go to a palace* not far from Broken Rainbow
Bridge for a bath every day. Each time she was accompanied by palace maids and eunuchs bearing palace
fans and censers as, like stars escorting the moon, they
saw her to her bath-house. Then they rested in the an-
nexes while she bathed. The Imperial Concubine liked
going there for a bath, and found nothing out of the
way. When she told the Emperor how much she enjoyed
this, he said:

"Then go and have a bath every day."

The Imperial Concubine went on bathing there every
day. The windows of her bath-house had glass panes,
but of course when she had her bath a strict watch was
kept and all the windows and doors were tightly shut.
Yet sometimes something strange happened. Exactly
when it started no one knows, but as time went by when
the concubine had her bath she seemed to see the faint
shadow of a little black figure on the window; yet when
she opened the window to look, there was no one there.
She took fright, but dared not tell the Emperor, for fear
he would forbid her to bath there in future. Instead,
she told her palace maids.

The palace maids said, "The palace is so big, and
has such a vast courtyard with all those old trees in it,
some evil spirits may manage to slip in. But don't be
afraid, madam. Once you've seen clearly what it is, just
call us and we'll nip out to catch it."

Strange to say, that small black shadow grew clearer
every day, scaring the Imperial Concubine more and

* The House of Bathing Virtue northwest of the Hall of Martial Valour. Qian Long's concubine Xiangfei, the Fragrant Concubine, was said to have bathed here, and the bath-house was
built in a Turkish style.

more. One day the strange shadow was not only clearer, she could even see it moving, reaching out its long scraggy arms as if to break through the window. In her panic she didn't stop to call her palace maids or the eunuchs, but snatched up a jade ladle and hurled it through the window. Crash! The glass was smashed and the little black shadow vanished.

The palace maids in the annexe hearing this ran out to see what had happened. They saw broken glass on the palace steps, and wondered who was responsible for this. When they went in to ask their mistress, they learned that she had thrown a ladle at the small black intruder.

"Hurry up and fetch that jade ladle back," the Imperial Concubine ordered. "It's a present from His Majesty, so see whether it is broken."

The palace maids went to make a search, but hunted

The Stone Monkeys on Broken Rainbow Bridge

high and low without finding the jade ladle. They were frantic. The Imperial Concubine, in desperation, sent for her eunuch attendants. When all eight of them had appeared, she told them of her loss and ordered them to go and find the jade ladle.

"That ladle was given me by the Emperor," she told them. "You've simply got to find it."

"Yes, madam!" the eunuchs chorused.

They searched in the hall and outside it, searched the whole courtyard. When they came to Broken Rainbow Bridge — ha! One of the stone monkeys on the balustrade had the jade ladle in his paw! But the ladle had stuck like a leech to the monkey, as if it had struck roots there, and try as they would they could not prize it loose. The eunuchs had to go back to report this to the Imperial Concubine.

Stamping her foot she cried, "What's to be done? If it were broken or chipped we could keep it hidden. But suppose the Emperor sees it in a stone monkey's paw, how am I to account for it? You fell down on your 'security', letting in a rascally monkey. You'll have your heads cut off!"

The eunuchs were frightened too. Together they thought up a plan. They had a yellow cloth cover made to slip over that monkey before the Emperor passed Broken Rainbow Bridge, so that he never noticed the jade ladle. That was the origin of this place of historic interest.

How Masted Vessels Passed Under Eight *Li* Bridge

THERE are many stories about the Grand Canal which links Beijing and Hangzhou, and here I shall tell you one from the Beijing district. The Grand Canal is over three thousand *li* long, but the stretch running eastwards from Beijing to Tongzhou is called the Inner Canal, and this is the subject of our story today.

The Inner Canal flows west from the North Gate of Tongzhou to Beijing's Dong Bian Men. Here the river is narrow and shallow, not to be compared with the deep-flowing Outer Canal. But the Old Emperor insisted on grain being shipped along it. Eight *li* to the west of Tongzhou a big stone bridge spans the Inner Canal, and everyone calls this Eight *Li* Bridge. How could rice boats pass under this bridge? But the Old Emperor insisted that pass they must! The rice boats on the Outer Canal all have tall pine masts, and are a fine sight under sail. But how could those high-masted rice boats sail through Eight *Li* Bridge or navigate the shallow, cramped Inner Canal? However, the Old Emperor issued an edict: Masted rice boats must pass through Eight *Li* Bridge. And in those days who dared disobey the Emperor? The boatmen on the Inner Canal were frantic. They sought out the shipwrights who built and repaired boats, and put their heads together.

If they failed to carry out the Emperor's orders, they would all be guilty of a crime and might even lose their heads. Anxiety put them off their food and sleep.

For two whole days they discussed how to get rice ships up the Inner Canal. Couldn't they use smaller boats than those on the Outer Canal, loading them with less rice? All agreed, "That's it! They'll still be rice boats, no matter how small they are!"

The second problem was how to get the rice boats under the bridge. This stumped them. One day then another went by, three days then four, and then they hit on a plan. When the boats reached Eight *Li* Bridge, they could ask the lock-keeper to let out less water, to lower the water under the bridge and make its archway higher. Then boats could go through, couldn't they? All agreed, "That's it! If the boats get through, we'll have carried out our orders."

The third problem seemed insurmountable. It was hard enough for rice boats to go under the bridge, but for masted boats it was surely impossible! How to find some way around this? One day then another went by, one month then another, and still they had hit on no plan. The Minister of Waterways was frantic. He sent for the boatmen and bellowed: "Do you all want to die? Grain from the Changjiang River (Yangzi) Valley will be coming in the autumn, and if the Emperor sees no white sails on the river you'll all lose your heads! I give you one month — no more — to make masted rice ships for the Inner Canal."

The boatmen agreed to this, and discussed ways and means with the ship-builders every day. One hot, sultry day, sitting on the river bank they felt not a breath of cool air.

"We can't think of any way out," they sighed. "And it's too stifling to eat. This anxiety's killing us!"

One boatman proposed, "Let's first eat some cold *hole* noodles. If we're to lose our heads tomorrow or the day after, that can't be helped."

The others said, "Yes, let's have a good meal of cold *hole* noodles first to cool us off."

The cook, a cheerful young fellow said, "I'll make noodles for you, mates, but you must all lend a hand."

"Of course," the others agreed. "We'll light the stove, work the bellows, supply the flour and knead the dough. You just make it into noodles."

The young cook set up his contraption for making noodles — a small wooden tub with round holes in its base and a piston above. He filled this with dough. Then — slap! — down came the piston, and the tray beneath filled with noodles. His mates forgot their worries in their eagerness to eat noodles. And the cook worked his piston merrily, singing out:

Who made my noodle tub so spick and span?
The long, long noodles splash into the pan;
The piston rises up and crashes down;
Lap up my noodles and your sorrows drown.

He was singing away when a ship-builder called out, "Hey, mates, don't start on those noodles yet. Hear him sing 'the piston rises up and crashes down'?"

"Yes, we heard him."

"Well, if we made masts like pistons, we could lower them to pass Eight Li Bridge, then raise them up again and hoist sail. Wouldn't that be a way to get masted vessels through?"

"Right you are!" cried the others, beaming. They

told the cook, "Hey, Master Lu Ban, stop making noodles. Come here."

The young cook roared with laughter and sang, "First fill up with noodles and then use your noddles!"

They all made a hearty meal of cold *hole* noodles, now that they had worked out how to make a movable mast.

Later on, no one knows what became of that young cook who liked to laugh and sing. But the story of how masted vessels passed under Eight *Li* Bridge was handed down. And story-tellers always end up by saying: Maybe that young cook was Lu Ban, or one of Lu Ban's sons or apprentices.

The Crescent Moon on the Tip of a Plum Tree

IN front of Beijing's Drum Tower outside Di An Men, the back gate of the Imperial City, is a lane called Hatters' Alley. In it stood a big temple, Illustrious Guardian Temple. No one troubles to ask what Buddha, what deity or what immortals were worshipped there. All we know is that this temple was pulled down scores of years ago, leaving no trace, and that there was once a stone carving here of a beautiful spray of plum blossom with a crescent moon on its tip. It was called the Crescent Moon on a Spray of Plum Blossom. Some say this was not carved on the stone by a sculptor but was a natural design in the smooth marble. But whatever it was, that stone tablet was thrown on the rubbish heap when the temple was pulled down. All that's left is this story which has come down to us.

Old, old people who tell this story have no idea when it was that there was a girl who loved to paint plum blossom. And they do not say where she lived or what her name was. All they know is that she was a Beijing girl. This girl devoted all her time to painting plum blossom. And because all who saw her paintings loved them and spoke highly of them, she was known as Plum Blossom Maid.

Plum Blossom Maid painted nothing but plum blos-

som, but had never painted plum blossom with a moon.
Why not? She thought: It would be fine to paint some
lovely white plum blossom with a crescent moon above
the tip of the bough! But all the plum-blossom and
moon paintings she had seen by old masters or famous
artists had a full moon behind the blossom, and she
objected to that. So she painted a spray of plum blossom with a crescent moon on its tip, which she really
loved. When she showed it to friends, though, they
pulled long faces and sighed:

"Ah, why paint a picture like that, Plum Blossom
Maid? This is different from the work of the old
masters or famous artists!"

Some said, "If Plum Blossom Maid goes on like this,
people won't like her paintings any more."

And indeed after that people stopped praising her
paintings, stopped admiring them and stopped men-
tioning her name. Still she loved this plum-blossom and
crescent moon painting. She hung it on her wall and
the more she looked at it the more she loved it. She
was convinced that this new way of painting of hers was
right.

As time went by, Plum Blossom Maid started feeling
worried. She asked herself, "Is it good or not, my
painting of plum blossom and a crescent moon? Is it
right?" She kept thinking the question over, but could
not make up her mind. One day she suddenly had an
idea and went cheerfully to tell her parents:

"Dad, mum! People don't like this plum blossom
and crescent moon of mine, do they? Maybe they don't
understand it. Maybe I've painted it badly. I want to
travel the country to see if there are other paintings like
this."

"You can't do that!" Her mother was horrified. "How can a girl travel the country?"

When Plum Blossom Maid persisted, her father said, "Very well then. You must get yourself up like a travelling scholar; then you can tour the country and have a look."

So Plum Blossom Maid slung a case of books over her shoulders, just like a travelling scholar, then left her parents to search far and wide for paintings of plum blossom and a crescent moon.

She travelled from place to place, from one village to another, and saw many paintings of plum blossom, including ones with a moon, but it was always a full moon behind the blossom. This made her feel more worried. She also went to see plum trees growing in dells or by the margin of lakes; but she never enjoyed the sight of a full moon behind the blossom. Why was this? She couldn't understand the reason.

One day she was travelling northwards when she overheard two men talking.

One said, "If a crescent moon were painted above a spray of plum blossom, how charming that would be. It's a pity no one realizes that."

His companion replied, "When I've time, I mean to go to Beijing to look for such a painting."

Plum Blossom Maid was staggered. Not until the two men had gone farther on did she take in what they had said and regret not having asked whereabouts in Beijing such a painting could be found. She turned her steps homeward and her spirits rose, her pace quickened, as she approached Beijing, the Eight-armed Nezha capital. But when she entered the city gate she had misgivings. How was she to find this painting in such a huge city? She walked the highways and byways searching the city.

One day she came to the gate of a big temple in the north city. Set in its wall was a plaque of white marble. At sight of it she stood rooted to the spot. Because on that white marble was a crescent moon above a spray of plum blossom, exactly like her painting. What did this mean? Plum Blossom Maid had no idea. As she was feasting her eyes on this, a white-bearded old man approached from the east, and she accosted him eagerly.

"Can you tell me, please, Old Uncle, who painted this exquisite plum blossom with a crescent moon?"

The old man eyed her shrewdly and then said, "Are you asking about this crescent moon and plum blossom, young scholar? This was painted by —" he indicated the board over the temple gate, "by the crazy Taoist of —Illustrious Guardian Temple."

Plum Blossom Maid looked up then at the golden characters hanging over the temple.

"If he paints so well, Old Uncle, why do you call him crazy?" she asked quickly.

"Of course he's crazy. In his teens he loved to paint plum blossom, and after a few years he painted this one with a crescent moon on the tip of the tree. Nobody liked it, yet that crazy Taoist insisted that it was good, better than a full moon behind the plum blossom."

Plum Blossom Maid thought: Why that's exactly like me! She hastily asked, "And for that you count him as crazy?"

"Of course. After painting this crescent moon on the tip of a plum tree that crazy Taoist waited stupidly for someone to admire it. He waited from the age of twenty to thirty, but nobody admired it. He waited from the

age of thirty to forty; still nobody admired it. Then in
desperation he carved this painting on marble and put
it up outside the gate of this temple, waiting for people
to come along and admire it. The crazy fellow waited
year after year for scores of years, till he turned eighty
yet still nobody admired this painting of his. That
really made the crazy Taoist frantic."

Plum Blossom Maid had listened raptly to this. Now
she felt frantic too and hurriedly asked, "What happened in the end to that crazy Taoist?"

The old man said with a smile, "Don't be so impatient, young scholar! The crazy Taoist waited sixty
whole years, from the age of twenty to eighty, yet
nobody had a good word to say about this crescent
moon over the plum tree. Of course that made him
frantic. So frantic that less than a year ago he died."

Because of what was preying on her own mind, Plum
Blossom Maid pitied the Taoist for his folly. She
stamped her foot and cried, "Ah poor Taoist priest! It's
too bad nobody could appreciate your painting."

Old White-beard roared with laughter and eyed her
shrewdly again. He said slowly, "I reckon you're a
painter yourself, young scholar. That crazy Taoist
didn't paint at all badly, but what's so wonderful about
a crescent moon on the tip of a plum tree? Plum blossom
grows in many different ways, and there are many different kinds of crescent moons, some waxing and some
waning — why didn't he paint more? He just stuck to
this one," he pointed at the carving on the marble slab.
"This one of a crescent moon on the tip of a plum tree.
He waited for people to praise him. So was he a crazy
Taoist or an intelligent Taoist?" Then, laughing again,
the old fellow walked away.

After listening to Old Whitebeard, Plum Blossom Maid had an inkling of his meaning. She glanced again at the plum tree and moon on the marble, then went home to go on painting. Since then this story about the moon on the tip of plum blossom in Illustrious Guardian Temple has come down from generation to generation.

北 京 的 传 说

金 受 申

熊 猫 丛 书

*

《中国文学》杂志社出版

（中国北京百万庄路24号）

中国国际图书贸易总公司发行

（中国国际书店）

外文印刷厂印刷

1982年第1版

1985年第2次印刷

编号：（英）2—916—11

00150

10—E—1620P